WRITE YOURSELF HAPPY

The Art of Positive Journalling

Megan C Hayes PhD

WRITE YOURSELF HAPPY

The Art of Positive Journalling

Megan C Hayes PhD

For my great-grandmother, Christine

An Hachette UK Company
www.hachette.co.uk

First published in Great Britain in 2018 by Gaia,
a division of Octopus Publishing Group Ltd
Carmelite House
50 Victoria Embankment
London EC4Y 0DZ
www.octopusbooks.co.uk
www.octopusbooksusa.com

Distributed in the US by
Hachette Book Group
1290 Avenue of the Americas
4th and 5th Floors
New York, NY 10104

Distributed in Canada by
Canadian Manda Group
664 Annette Street
Toronto, Ontario, Canada M6S 2C8

ISBN 978 1 85675 382 1

A CIP catalogue record for this book is available from the British Library.

Printed and bound in China

1 3 5 7 9 10 8 6 4 2

Commissioning Editor   Leanne Bryan
Art Director   Yasia Williams-Leedham
Senior Editor   Alex Stetter
Designer   Nicky Collings
Production Controller   Dasha Miller

Picture acknowledgements
Lera Efremova/Shutterstock; Lidia Kubrak/Shutterstock.

CONTENTS

INTRODUCTION

This is a book about writing and how it can make us happier. It is not about grammar, sentence structure or how to create atmosphere in our prose. It is about the psychology behind writing things down and how a technique called positive journalling can enable us find joy, serenity, contentment and much more.

Do you keep a diary or a journal? Have you ever written more in it than a list of appointments or reminders? Did you keep a diary as a teenager and regret that you dropped the practice as you became older and busier? Have you been bitten by the creative journalling bug and have a beautifully embellished grid journal in which you artfully set out your plans for today, tomorrow, next year? If so, you are in good company. Perhaps as a backlash to our feverish, digital world, more of us are keeping journals than ever before. Journal writing also has a long and distinguished history. Think of the great London chronicler Samuel Pepys, or the philosopher Jean-Jacques Rousseau and his *Confessions*, or the diarists Virginia Woolf and Anaïs Nin... The list goes on.

Many of the greatest minds in history were avid journal writers, but having a great mind is not a prerequisite of writing in a journal. Whoever we *are*, journal writing can serve as a map of *who we are becoming*. It is a record of what has happened to us, how we have experienced it and what we did with that experience.

YOUR JOURNAL IS A TOOL
FOR LIVING LIFE WELL

For this reason, how we go about journal writing – the art of journalling – is particularly important, but most of us tend not to think much about this. For some of us, journalling is only about setting and achieving goals. For others, it is about organizing our time. In my work, I have seen that many people instinctively treat diaries or journals as a place to vent or unload difficult feelings – anger, frustration, resentment and grief.

What this book offers is an entirely new way to look at journalling. In its pages I am inviting you to discover and to try out a method of writing called *positive journalling*. It offers a roadmap for using your journal as more than just a place to stringently manage your time or to deposit your negative emotions; it shows you how your journal can become a space in which to uncover and explore your most positive emotions, and enable you to thrive as a result. This book invites you to see writing as a powerful tool to help you feel fulfilled, every day. In other words, to use writing in order to be happy.

As for me, although my first passion has always been writing, the topics of happiness and wellbeing have never been far from my mind. I grew up in a family where those closest to me encountered mental ill health. For this reason I have always been curious about the age-old questions that have preoccupied humanity: what does it mean to be happy? What is a good life? How can we be optimistic – and is this even important – in a sometimes dire world? After I had completed my first degree in Creative Writing, these questions took me to a further degree in Applied Positive Psychology – the scientific study of happiness and wellbeing. I wondered, could science hold the answers?

If writing when things go wrong can help us, what happens if we write when things go right?

It was then that I made a discovery that saw my two passions – writing and wellbeing – fuse. For decades, scientists had been making remarkable breakthroughs on the topic of how writing can help people overcome trauma and challenges. Writing about difficult experiences, they had found, could bring about not only emotional health benefits, but physical health benefits too. If writing when things go wrong can help us, I wondered, what happens if we write when things go right? Might writing help us, not only to be less sad, but – more than this – to be happy, in a way that bolsters us for challenges to come? This book and the research behind it are the results of these questions.

I set out to uncover how writing through the lens of our most positive emotions might make us happier, and was amazed by what I found. I called this project The Positive Journalling Study.[1] In the first part of this book I will share these findings with you, and then we will move on to the individual positive emotions that can help get you started in positive journalling, including joy, gratitude, serenity, interest, hope, pride, awe and love. In the chapters devoted to each of these feelings, you will find practical exercises and a host of ideas that will enable you to use your own experiences to access these feel-good emotions and make a step toward change in your life.

Of course, in the end, science can only tell us so much about the messy reality of being human. Journalling, too, is an individual, creative, messy and sometimes random art form. I am not suggesting that positive journalling is a cure-all or a miracle ointment – it is not. What I do believe, and what I hope you will discover in this book, is that positive journalling is an extremely versatile and enjoyable tool that can have a profound effect on your wellbeing. My hope is simply that in reading this book you will gather some tips that will make your journal a happier place to spend time, and will enhance your life a little along the way.

Writing is such a strikingly simple act. It does not require you to have great literary ability or even particularly advanced literacy, even though it can benefit from this. It does not require that you possess much money, or any tools beyond a scrap of paper and the nub of a pencil. Yet, for these small demands, the benefits can be vast. Whether you have never written in a journal or diary or are a seasoned pro, this book will help you write more positively, in order to see positive changes in your life.

Let's begin.

WHAT POSITIVE JOURNALLING IS

and how it can help us to thrive

Positive journalling is a fun and adaptable writing practice that fuses two fascinating areas of science: writing and positive psychology. Writing, in various forms, has been empirically studied and shown to have many beneficial effects upon diverse areas of our lives. The field of positive psychology, often called the science of happiness, has shown that simple, positive changes in our lives can have a profound effect on our wellbeing. Positive journalling combines these two, creating a powerful practice that offers us the opportunity to write ourselves happier – every day.

An important feature of positive journalling is that this kind of writing is almost effortlessly *doable*. If you can put pen to paper and string a sentence together, or type on a keyboard – and if you can spare just ten or twenty minutes a day – then you can benefit from the practice of *positive* journalling. This book will show you exactly how to get to grips – quickly and easily – with using this practice in your own life.

But before we begin our journey into positive journalling, we might want to think about some very basic questions. What does it mean to be positive? Is it the same thing as happiness? If it is, then is happiness just a happy accident – with some people simply innately more chirpy than others? Or can we actively cultivate positivity, even in a world of ever-increasing statistics of depression?

If you can put pen to paper
and string a sentence together,
or type on a keyboard,
then you can benefit quickly
from the practice of
positive journalling.

POSITIVITY AND WHY IT MATTERS

With these questions in mind, think about another question: what if we do not get sad and feel hopeless because we are depressed, but we get depressed because we feel sad and hopeless? This is exactly what some positive psychologists have suggested. Scientists such as Martin Seligman, who is often called the "father" of positive psychology, believe that a lack of positive feelings might not always be just a symptom of depression, *but its cause.*[2] This means that if you invest in your positivity, you might be giving yourself your own figurative flu jab against depression.

This is not to say you must strive to be perpetually cheerful. Emotional ups and downs are, of course, absolutely normal in human beings. It is good news, though. Positive psychology shows us that even the most seemingly simple changes in our lives can have a big impact, making us more resilient, creative and engaged in the face of life's challenges. We can, in many ways, cultivate our own positivity.

For a long time, scientists did not think this way. Positive emotions, historically speaking, were not felt to be the "important" emotions, particularly from an evolutionary perspective. Our *happier* emotions, apparently, were not a serious or rigorous enough topic of study! Instead, psychologists emphasized the great importance of emotions such as disgust and fear. They argued that our ancestors developed these emotions for highly practical reasons, so that they would not do or eat anything that would cause them harm. This is true: disgust and fear are important emotions, but now scientists have begun to wonder whether our positive emotions might not be equally practical. Early humans were not likely to survive if they scaled icy cliff faces without a care in the world, or gorged themselves on poisonous plants; but, similarly, they were not very likely to survive if they did not bond with others, experience a sense of awe and curiosity to learn more about their world, or satisfy their remarkably big, questioning brains that this mad and often catastrophic life was worth living with a sense of pride, or hope for the future.

The truth is that negative and positive emotions alike are integral to human nature. Positive emotions, *across millennia*, have played a key part in helping us build resources for our survival. Imagine a gang of listless, lonely and depressed cave people – none of them striving to feed and protect their loved ones, or stick around a while, or ponder with interest what might happen if they sharpened that stone into a tool... Luckily, this isn't how it was, and the rest, as they say, is history.

Despite many hundreds of leading psychologists changing their minds about positivity, it is still a topic that is often, and unfairly, portrayed as flippant and superfluous. In reality, our positive emotions, far from being frivolous pastimes, are some of the most profound tools for survival we have ever had in our arsenal. Why might this matter to modern life? Well, for one, most of us are at least a little bit interested in being better people – kinder, more resilient, more productive, at peace with others and ourselves. Simply put: we want to grow. Almost 20 years of research in positive psychology have shown that positive emotions act as engines of personal growth, not only as a pleasant side effect of life (we will get to this a little later).[3] More than this, it is a sad-but-true fact that humans are increasingly depressed by modern life. Depression has even been called a world health crisis. Can we shield ourselves against depression by experiencing or "self-generating" positive emotions? Many researchers in positive psychology believe we can.

It was thinking about all this that led me to design The Positive Journalling Study and to write this book. Writing is a powerful tool that we humans have long used to give shape to our emotions.

Positive journalling is about using the page to prioritize our most treasured, uplifting emotions – but the science of *writing ourselves well* has not always promoted this. Researchers have tended to focus not on writing to be happier when things are OK, but writing to heal when things go wrong. This is also a powerful way to write, so we will take a quick look at it now, before we look at how positive journalling is different.

THE SCIENCE OF WRITING OURSELVES WELL

A great deal of scientific research into what is called *expressive writing* has shown us that writing about challenging experiences – from job loss to heartbreak to living with cancer – can have remarkable effects on both our emotional and physical health.[4] This fascinating research has shown us the profound ways that writing can *heal* – but what if there were much more to writing than helping us to heal when things go wrong?[5] Can we also pen our greatest hopes, our joys and our interests – and make constructive change beyond simply coping? Might writing help us, not only to survive in the tough times, but also to thrive in the good?

There have been a few studies in recent years on more positive ways of writing. Some have combined expressive writing with the recent trend toward mindfulness,[6] suggesting that those who are more mindful might benefit more from writing. Others have encouraged writing about "intensely positive experiences".[7] Another positive version of expressive writing is called "benefit-finding"[8] – encouraging the writer to reframe a trauma in optimistic terms by focusing on the positive outcomes of troubling experiences, such as illness. Interestingly, this can be just as effective as typical expressive writing.

These more positive forms of expressive writing show us that the practice of writing is infinitely adaptable. They also show us that, even if we are experiencing challenges, going headfirst at them in our writing may not always be the most comforting or helpful approach. We might want to write, instead, with *hope* for better times ahead. Or we might focus on finding some *serenity*, accepting that every life involves suffering. This idea is at the heart of positive journalling: we can take advantage of research in positive psychology in our writing, but *still feel the freedom to express ourselves*, and whatever we are going through, openly on the page.

WRITING OUR POSITIVE EMOTIONS

Positive journalling can help us to combine all of the research we have looked at so far – including mindfulness and benefit-finding – but it also goes a step beyond this, to create a more holistic, everyday writing practice. At the centre of any positive journalling practice are some vital building blocks: our positive emotions.

Expressing our emotions is integral to writing for wellbeing. The results of the very earliest expressive writing study in the 1980s showed that writing the facts of a trauma alone did not offer the greatest benefits for participants.[9] Those who wrote about the trauma *and* the emotions they felt in relation to it were the ones to experience the most profound results.

Expressing our emotions is integral to writing for wellbeing.

What about our *positive* emotions – are they really that important? Well, psychologists tell us that, when we feel positive, we are kinder and tend to get along with each other a lot better.[10] Feeling positive can help us to connect with others, often because it softens our defences and biases.[11] More than this, regular feelings of positive emotion have been shown to promote our resilience.[12] Positive psychologist Barbara Fredrickson at the University of North Carolina has suggested that feeling positive emotions, in comparison with negative ones, helps to *broaden* our minds to encompass a wider range of thoughts and potential actions. This expansive feature of positivity spurs what Fredrickson calls an *upward spiral*, where we are prompted to build practical, social and psychological resources. This is known as Fredrickson's broaden-and-build theory of positive emotions.[13] Positivity, apparently, is a veritable multivitamin for our wellbeing.

How might all this be applied to our journal writing? For starters, some psychologists have shown that when writers use positive emotion words such as *happiness*, *enthusiasm* or *amusement* in what they write, the benefits of the writing appear to be greater.[14] Clearly, then, writing in a way that might encourage greater positivity – and genuine expression of this positivity – seems like a good practice to get into. Rather than focusing on our challenges alone, writing with our positive emotions might have a whole host of benefits over and above those of typical expressive writing, which focuses on our challenges.

This is exactly why The Positive Journalling Study came about. It was designed to offer the "lens" of positive emotions in writing – to highlight these emotions – yet *without limiting what we could write about*. From the science, what seems most important about writing is the *way* we write, not the content. Expressing ourselves honestly and fluidly is much more vital in writing ourselves happier than fixating only on a certain happy topic.

THE POSITIVE JOURNALLING STUDY

The Positive Journalling Study explored what happens when we alter the way we practise writing in a journal – not only waiting for misery to strike and "offloading" our dark emotions onto the page as the early blues musicians did with their guitars, but becoming actively motivated by positive emotions in our writing. As it turns out, writing this way appears to offer a whole range of extra benefits from the humble pen and paper than simple catharsis.

The study was based on the most common positive emotions we experience, including joy, gratitude, serenity, interest, hope, pride, awe and love. The people in the study chose from these emotions each day, and used them in their journals over three days. They were then invited to share their experiences of this positive journalling in interviews.

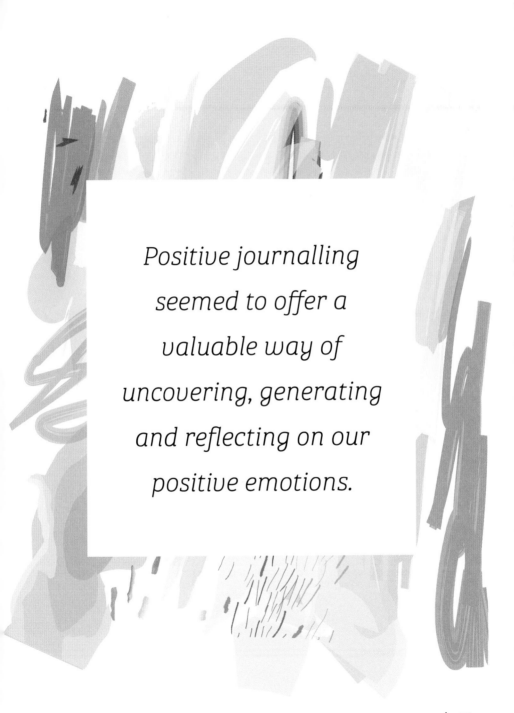

Positive journalling seemed to offer a valuable way of uncovering, generating and reflecting on our positive emotions.

THE THREE BENEFITS OF POSITIVE JOURNALLING

I was excited by the results of the study. They showed that positive journalling seemed to offer a valuable way of uncovering, generating and reflecting on our positive emotions. In addition to alleviating our bad feelings, this way of writing could help us cultivate our *great* feelings, harnessing these emotions in order to power us along our individual journeys toward self-growth. According to the results of the study, this worked in three key ways:

1 WE FEEL DIRECTED.

Typical responses to positive journalling were about feeling there was a bit more "control" or structure to the writing, compared with "normal" journalling. Participants said their writing felt related, directed and anchored, whereas they previously had the "urge" to write when things – typically negative things – were "going round and round and round" in their head. Doing so would help to "get the stuff out of the way" or "download" it onto the page, so that they could go and do something else instead. This often meant that the writing was somewhat chaotic, urgent and almost against the writer's will. When we write difficult things down, we do sometimes feel much better – but these chaotic, scribbled pages may leave us feeling lost. Positive journalling offers a guided path through this personal material, helping us feel a little more in control.

2 WE CHANGE OUR PERSPECTIVES.

People felt that positive journalling enabled them to write about things in a new way, from a fresh perspective that surprised them, but was still deeply reflective. They noted that they had normally been driven to journal about what was bothering them, which often meant that they were writing the same negative things over and over again. Focusing on positive emotions offers a profoundly new way to look at the events of our lives – bringing to our attention resources that we may never have noticed before.

3 WE DO MORE THAN REACT TO WHAT HAPPENS.

Those who took part in the study tended to feel that they had actively gained something from the writing; they described feeling more capable, and as though they had made progress, rather than just having the impetus to write when they were not feeling good. Positive journalling encourages us to focus on our ability to change our circumstances and to make progress in our lives – not only to write knee-jerk responses to negative situations, such as having had a tiresome day.

These findings probably only scratch the surface of the vital role positive emotions can play in our journal writing – but they are nevertheless intriguing, and offer a lot of encouragement to try out positive journalling for ourselves. Journalling-as-usual is a way of *processing* the events of our lives, whereas positive journalling appears to offer us a fulfilling sense of *progressing* in life.

One person in the study, Rose, said that in her positive journalling she was not only "thinking about flowers and hearts and nice clouds" but was positively assessing her experiences, and this made her feel better about several areas of her life. Compare this to Laura, who said that her journalling-as-usual had been "a place to download or offload a lot of negative feelings, a lot of difficulties, which were just repetitive". Positive journalling is not about being superficially upbeat – it offers a way to reflect on and understand our lives in novel and surprisingly helpful ways. The study showed that we can feel actively *good* and proactive about our lives in our writing, not only relieved or less bad. Positive journalling can prevent us from replaying the negative, and enable us to make more constructive assessments about our lives. This is a strikingly different approach to an already very powerful tool.

Perhaps the results of the study ring true for you. When we write in a journal, it is easy to slip into using it as a form of relief. We hear advice to this effect all the time: writing is a way to "clear our minds" by "getting it out" on the page. This might often be necessary – crucial, even – and what a wonderful tool journalling is to have at our disposal to do just this when times are hard. Yet what The Positive Journalling Study shows is that there is much more to writing. Writing can offer us a way, not only to process the event of our lives, but to feel we are making progress.

Positive journalling offers a way to reflect on and understand our lives in novel and surprisingly helpful ways.

HOW POSITIVE JOURNALLING CAN HELP YOU

It is now time to get stuck in and begin your own positive journalling journey. Grab a notebook, or write some notes on this page, and think about your answers to the following:

1

WHAT IF YOUR JOURNAL WRITING WAS MORE DIRECTED?

This might mean a kind of aspirational writing, making the page a place to build resources – such as confidence, compassion or wisdom – rather than only to heal what is hurting. As fictional psychiatrist Jennifer Melfi says in the HBO series *The Sopranos*, if you spend all your time putting out fires, there is little time to help things grow. Once the fire is out, writing in a journal may still have far more to offer us. What do you want to help grow in your life, using journalling?

2

WHAT IF YOU QUESTIONED YOUR PERSPECTIVES IN YOUR JOURNAL?

If you already keep a journal, look back over recent entries and ponder if your perspectives have been helping you or if perhaps they have been holding you back. If you have not written before, positive journalling might be a way to turn around some unhelpful ideas you have been holding onto. Are there any limiting perspectives you might change through positive journalling?

WHAT IF YOU DID MORE THAN JUST REACT IN YOUR JOURNAL?

Do you simply respond to what happens to you in life by writing it down? Would you prefer to actively engage with it, reinterpret it and attempt to change it? Should you challenge yourself to think differently? This is another remarkable advantage that positive journalling has over the simple relief of journalling-as-usual: it puts the power back in your own hands, because it highlights how you are interpreting your life. Sometimes, writing through the lens of a positive emotion may feel strange and awkward. You may think, "My experience does not belong here." Yet – what if it did belong? Interact with your experience a little. Poke it and prod it and see what different interpretations you might make. This is not about shoehorning hard times under the label "happiness". It is about asking questions of your experience; checking if the interpretation you have is serving you, or others, and how you might deal with a situation differently.

HOW TO APPROACH
THE POSITIVE EMOTIONS
IN THIS BOOK

The chapters to come outline eight specific emotions that you can use in your positive journalling practice, and offer ways for you to begin writing with them. These emotions are not offered as an exhaustive list of the ways you can experience positivity in your writing – not by half! Instead, think of them as a first step into writing with some of your most cherished – and most often experienced – positive emotions. In fact, positive emotions are only the beginning of how you can use a positive journal. If you are ready to start writing, jump ahead to page 57; if you want to explore more of the potentials of a positive journalling practice, stick with me for this next chapter. There we will have a look at the wide-ranging ways in which we might make use of positive journalling – and cover a few things to keep in mind when getting started.

PUTTING POSITIVE PSYCHOLOGY INTO PRACTICE

All of us have, at some point, probably written resolutions for the New Year, set ourselves monthly or weekly goals, or jotted daily to-do lists. We do these things because they serve a function: to motivate us toward getting stuff done and putting our highest aspirations into practice. We all know, however, that these techniques do not always work. Resolutions in particular can often leave us feeling worse about ourselves than before. Their incompletion seems to cement the fact that we really are, as we secretly suspected, just bunglingly inept and lazy. This is one reason why positive journalling should not be confused with simple goal-setting. Positive journalling is different; it is a constructive practice in and of itself, not merely a means to an end. This chapter is about why and how the practice of positive journalling is different.

Positive journalling

is a hands-on, simple

and versatile tool.

BROADENING THE SCOPE OF POSITIVE JOURNALLING

Positive psychology is a relatively young field. The questions it asks, however, are perennial – drawing upon ancient philosophy, as well as over a century of psychological research. Positive psychology therefore explores some of the longest-held aspirations of human beings – yet adds a new, more scientific flavour to these age-old questions. Perhaps you have heard of studies on *character strengths*, or the benefits of having a *growth mindset*, or even the concept of *self-compassion*. These are all intriguing parts of positive psychology. Yet it is sometimes tricky to know how to put this remarkable research into practice in the nooks and crannies of our daily lives.

I believe this fascinating science should not sit stagnantly in textbooks. We should put it to *use* in our daily lives – and *hurrah!* – positive journalling offers a way to do just this. We can, if we choose, embrace this way of writing as something much broader than a single scientific study. It is a hands-on, simple and versatile tool for putting positive psychology, in all its manifestations, into practice. The science is important – but it is action that really matters. As psychologist and writing researcher, James Pennebaker, has suggested it is important that we try writing on for size to see how it fits, rather than adopt research findings as a hard-and-fast set of rules.[15] So let us be galvanized into trying out positive journalling ourselves and experimenting with it, to see how it best works for us.

Whenever you come across the latest scientific "breakthrough" on the topic of happiness, think: how can I put this into practice using my journal? This simple question can actually be infinitely empowering. It takes happiness out of the hands of those in the white lab coats, and back into daily life where it belongs. It puts us in charge of our own wellbeing. This is profoundly important, because happiness has so many shades and so many unique subtexts for each of us, that we should be wary of even using that one word "happiness" to cover it all. Positive journalling is a way to explore the many shades of happiness.

THE MANY SHADES OF HAPPINESS – AND WHY THEY ARE IMPORTANT

We use a lot of words for our sadness: grumpy, melancholy, glum, blue, down, gutted, low, miserable, gloomy... When it comes to positivity, however, we are often a lot less specific – vague, even. Someone asks how we are, and, especially in Britain, even if things are going well we respond with "not bad", "OK" or "same old". Even if we do want to be notably positive and refer to our wellbeing, we tend to default to that one word, *happy*, to cover it all.

Most of us would say we know what it looks like to be happy. We picture a child at a birthday party. Perhaps we envisage their elation and rainbow sugar sprinkles on sticky cheeks. Yet this is just one shade of happiness. Over the coming chapters, we will take a look at eight of the most frequently felt positive emotions. We will do this because each of these emotions is a puzzle piece of a much bigger picture. The premise of this book, and of positive journalling, is this: happiness is not only sugar sprinkles. Happiness is something overarching. Happiness is not a prize that we are awarded when the conditions of our lives become miraculously perfect. Happiness is a *practice*.

The premise of positive journalling is this: happiness is not only sugar sprinkles. Happiness is something overarching.

Some of us misinterpret happiness as perpetual chirpiness, or something verging on naivety. If we do, then at best we disregard it and at worst we are actually enraged by the idea that we should seek to be happy – because the concept of happiness becomes unrealistic, vague or even insipid for us. This view conveniently ignores the fact that even the happiest life will, of course, include setbacks and struggles. Happiness must not be whitewashed; it has as many hues as our melancholy. When did you last feel in awe, for example? Or interested? Joyful? Proud? These emotions – happy emotions – are the privilege of all of us. My own research has shown how little we tend to take note of these nuances in our positivity. This is a great shame, because positivity is about much more than simply a hedonistic brand of feeling good.

HOW OUR EMOTIONS GET US MOVING

Positive emotions are integral to the human condition, our growth as individuals and the binding of empathetic, altruistic societies. Yet, more and more in modern society, our positive emotions are quashed or misdirected. They are accosted by soft-drink advertisements or held hostage by mobile-phone apps. Rather than deep bonds, we seek the fast thrills of swiping yes or no to potential dates. Rather than thoughtful awe at the majesty of the shape-shifting sky above us, we direct our gaze downward for the dopamine hit of confectionery-based games on our smart phones. As a result, we may question happiness, scrutinize it with a cynical glare: why, we demand, is happiness important in this world-gone-mad – a world of profound suffering, deceitful politicians and environmental crisis? Is apathy or distrust not a more valid response? One vital reply to this question is that positive emotions *mobilize* us.

Have you ever thought about the origins of the word "emotion"? It comes from the 16th-century French word *émotion* meaning "a (social) moving, stirring, agitation" and from the older French *emouvoir*, which meant "to stir up". Our emotions, both literally and figuratively, "move" us. Fear and disgust move us *away*; joy and awe move us *toward*. If we are afraid, we cower or we run from what we fear. If we are hopeful or joyful, we forge forward. We live in a world that, more and more, needs us to move forward. Toward each other, toward revolution, toward change... And our positive emotions are at the core of this. Being fed up is one thing, but being fed up and fearful? Well, that just leaves us sitting indoors, picking angrily at the threads of our armchairs while the evil behemoths of the world triumph. Being fed up and *hopeful*, or fed up and *interested*, or fed up and in *awe* at grassroots community spirit – now there are some powerful combinations.

More and more in modern society, our positive emotions are quashed or misdirected. We may question happiness, scrutinize it with a cynical glare.

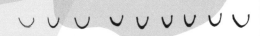

THE POWER
OF THE PEN

One of the reasons, among many, that we are often vague about our positive emotions is that they are so fleeting and seemingly insubstantial. They might last minutes, seconds even – and then we forget all about them and hurry on with whatever we were doing, like taking out the rubbish or clicking half-heartedly at our work computer. Negative emotions, on the other hand, can be overwhelming. Often we cannot help but verbalize negative emotions because it is the only way we can gain some semblance of control in the utterly incoherent swamp of grief or fury. This is potentially why the people in The Positive Journalling Study typically found themselves driven to write when things went wrong and tended to forget completely when things went right – they were too busy having fun!

Of course, no one would suggest that in the miracle moment of positivity you down tools and run off to a corner to scribble the details in your journal. We can probably all agree that that would be ridiculous. However, after the event, we can reflect on and savour these positive emotional experiences. We can find words for their complexity, give shape and structure to their minutiae. This is the power of the pen: it gives concreteness to emotional experience. What we capture in a journal we get to rediscover – to *relive*, to a certain extent. One group of scientists found, through a series of studies about journal writing, that even though keeping a record of everyday events might at first appear inconsequential, rediscovering moments we may otherwise have forgotten can make us feel good – like a present we are gifting to our future selves. One person who took part in these studies said, "Re-reading this event of doing mundane stuff with my daughter has certainly brightened my day. I'm glad I chose that event to write about because of the incredible joy it gives me at this moment."[16] Rediscovering buried or otherwise overlooked moments of positivity is one of the ideas at the heart of positive journalling.

POSITIVE JOURNALLING: THE BASICS

Hopefully you are now raring to go with positive journalling as a way to put positive psychology into practice, explore all the shades of your happiness and use the power of the pen to capture and relive the best bits of your life. On the following pages you will find a few basics for getting started. If you are a first-time journal writer, the aim of these fundamentals is to encourage you to feel confident in beginning to write from scratch. If you are more seasoned in journalling, think of them as a refresher.

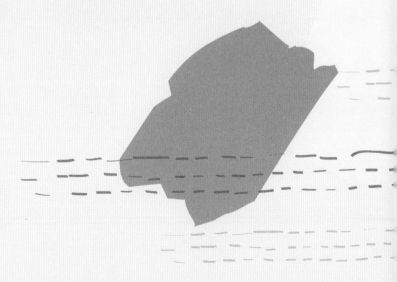

TOOLS

It seems so simple: to keep a journal all you need is a writing tool (pen, pencil, nub of a purple crayon) and something to write on (paper, a notepad, a coffee-shop napkin). And, yes, it is really that simple. However, we humans have a way of taking seemingly simple things and tying ourselves in knots over them. Our brains can definitely do this with journalling. We talk ourselves out of it because we agonize over what to write, whether it will read well, whether our handwriting is neat enough and whether we will "mess up" that gorgeous cloth-bound journal by besmirching it with our crude contemplations. All of these undermine the fundamental point of writing in a journal, which is to be openly and honestly reflective and expressive. You cannot be genuinely expressive if you are worried about saying the "wrong" thing or about making a mess of a special journal. So, henceforth, let the tools of journalling meet this one standard and one standard alone: *writing tools should facilitate our writing practice.*

If a fancy journal seizes you up in panic because it raises the stakes of your writing, then do not use a fancy journal. If an engraved fountain pen sends you into frenzy because you think your handwriting is terrible, then do not use an engraved fountain pen. If you abhor writing by hand and want to tap a journal into your laptop or other device, then that is a better option than not journalling at all. With this rule in mind, you will probably find that the tools that best facilitate your writing are the backs of bus tickets, receipts or coupon stubs, all written frantically in spider scrawl with the old chewed-up ballpoint pen from the bottom of your bag. Either that, or you have to forgive yourself in advance for making a "mess" of an elegant journal. That mess is called life. If forgiveness or a stubby pencil or a yellow legal pad is what it takes to journal honestly, freely and in abundance, then they are all the tools you need.

TIMING

When and how often should you keep a journal? Simply put, there are no *shoulds*. Writing is only useful insofar as it is useful to you. Yes, you might do well to write regularly, because otherwise it is an easy thing to brush over and forget to do altogether. But *shoulds*? They shrivel enthusiasm. They leach the joy out of the act. The more fun we find in an activity, the more we will do it. It is funny how that works. So if you really want a *should*, then it is this: you should aim for your positive journalling to be as much fun as possible, so that you find you actually want to do it. Write first thing, along with a cosy cup of tea and blissful quiet. Or do it to pass the time on the train to work as you watch the world whizz by the window. Do it in the bathtub (warning: logistical nightmare) if that is the only time you get to yourself. Or do it last thing at night, even if you only manage 30 seconds before your droopy eyelids betray you. Do it once a month, or three times a day – every chance you can manufacture or whenever the opportunity arises. What matters, really, is not the timing, but a tender tenacity.

TASKS

What are you going to write in your journal? Should you stick to prescribed exercises or go for freestyle inky outbursts? The answer is both! Or either! Or neither! Are you sensing a theme here? Do whatever works for you. We often only find out what works for us through experimentation, because many of us have misguided views about what we think we will enjoy. So try to test your boundaries a little. If you are someone who loves to free-write without any prepared exercise, then try a few set writing tasks – like the ones dotted through this book. If free-writing terrifies you and you like the rigidity of a prescribed task, test your boundaries with some short 30-second free-writes, starting with only a brief prompt such as "hope". You could also merge the two by designing your own writing prompts or tasks. Make up your own exercises in advance by writing them on slips of paper and keeping them in a box or jar for when you next sit down to write. These could be as simple as thinking up a few themes, like "New Beginnings", "Misunderstandings" or "Journeys", which you can write about through the lens of any of the emotions in this book. You could also – as was proposed at the start of this chapter – look to the broader field of positive psychology for ideas on how to journal positively. Think up some ways to write your strengths or to write with self-compassion. Allow yourself to enjoy the trial and error of journal writing, because it is only through this process that you will find out which approaches will truly work best for you.

BREAKING OUT OF SELF-CENSORSHIP IN YOUR JOURNAL

A final important point – whichever tools, timings or tasks you choose for your journal practice – is to keep a check on *self-censorship*. When keeping a journal it can be challenging to be completely honest with yourself. This may be because you imagine a future reader who might judge you, or because you have an internalized critic making snide comments about your poor penmanship, sloppy grammar or lack of noteworthy life experiences. Quieting the self-censor is nevertheless a skill you can develop and a way of making your journal writing increasingly fulfilling. If you know that this is something you struggle with, try journalling on loose sheets of paper, promising yourself you can destroy them later. You may find that you do in fact have the courage to bind and keep these pages, or you may not – but the practice is valid in either case, as it is a way to develop your capacity for candour.

You may also like to begin with the words "If I were to be really honest with myself here, I would write that…" and then see what follows. When you come to a natural end, begin again: "If I were to be even more honest with myself here, I would write that…" Repeat until you sense you have truly expressed what is going on for you. Do not be afraid to contradict yourself. Feel free to stop and begin again, perhaps even writing "No, I wasn't truly being honest there, what I really want to say is…" This can be a powerful manner of breaking away from self-censorship. Once this level of open expression becomes more natural to you, you may feel able to gravitate back to a bound journal, maintaining something of the same sincerity.

If you like the idea of a later generation happening across your journal as a historical relic, and so find yourself editing your authentic experiences to something you think is more palatable for these imagined descendants, consider this: when have you felt the most connected, inspired or comforted by another person? Was it when they were communicating to you in a clipped, censored manner or when they were being candid and forthcoming about the struggles or embarrassments they have endured, with which you yourself could empathize? For most of us, it is the latter. Your journal is more than just a highlight reel, even if you are committed to making it a highly positive practice, and leaving only a highlight reel is unlikely to truly enamour and engage a later reader. Give any future inheritor of your journal the gift of an honest account of how you lived: warts, wonders and all.

HOW TO NAVIGATE THE CHAPTERS THAT FOLLOW

There you have the basics of positive journal writing. Hopefully they will help, even if only to allow you to see that you need not take journalling too seriously. This style of writing is a practical and enjoyable tool to use in whatever way might serve you best.

Having covered these basics, it is finally time to roll up those sleeves, brandish those pens and smooth open a fresh journal page (or bus ticket). It is time to begin your very own positive journalling practice.

Each of the chapters that follow will offer a different positive emotion to write with. You do not have to read these in order – you may prefer simply to dip in and out of them, depending on which emotion speaks to you on a given day. Every chapter ends with a list of practical exercises, so you can always jump ahead to get writing, or pause to read a little about the psychology behind each emotion. The choice is yours.

Let's get started.

Writing

Joy

Words can evoke many things. We have all had the experience of being deeply engrossed in a storybook – it feels as if we are actually there. We smell the pine of the forbidden forest. We hear the crowd noise and taxi horns of a New York City street corner. We feel our feet sink in the mud and the piercing heat of a gunshot on the battlefield. Few of us would argue that books and stories can move us deeply, make us feel and experience the whole world from the comfort of a cosy chair by the fire.

The words we write can also transport us in this way and, in this sense, they can help us to self-generate the emotions we are writing.

Which words, scenes, incidents or ways of writing might evoke joy for you? There are no strict rules for writing with positive emotions, so this chapter and the ones that follow will serve only as beginners' guides to each emotion. The most important part of writing with positive emotions is for it to feel sincere. That is why this book offers eight different emotions – one might fit on a certain day and not at all on another. Joy might be an appropriate emotion to write if it has just been your birthday and you are surrounded by your loved ones, yet not at all if your job is on the line or your partner has just become ill.

We must always feel free to write life as it is happening to us: to write our most genuine feelings without having to filter ourselves. If not, we would not be able to call this kind of writing *expressive*, but rather a sort of far-fetched invention that makes life look eternally rosy. This would not be any help to us at all. In fact, emotionally speaking, it would probably make us feel worse. Heartfelt sincerity is the name of the game when it comes to positive journalling, so offer yourself the patience, compassion and curiosity to uncover this sincerity as you begin your practice.

THE PSYCHOLOGY OF JOY

Psychologists tell us that joy emerges when we experience good fortune, like some great news or a lovely surprise – and that joy sparks within us the impulse to be playful.[17] This may be a useful definition for you, or it may not. Importantly, in order to feel you are being authentically expressive in your positive journalling, you should feel a genuine connection to the emotions with which you write. Therefore you should acknowledge the fact that *how* you experience any given emotion – or cocktail of emotions – is often kaleidoscopically unique.

One person might feel joy suddenly, in a gleeful burst, whereas another might experience it as a slow, building sensation when a lot of things appear to be going right at once. Another person might associate it with the sun shining, time spent with a special friend or arriving home after a long day. Perhaps for you it is that sensation when you cannot help but smile, or when you feel a rush of endorphins through every limb. The most important thing when writing with positive emotions is that the emotions authentically chime with you. With that in mind, take a moment now to write your own precise description of joy. I encourage you to do this with all of the emotions in the chapters to come.

Joy appears to have one thing in common for most of us, and that is how it makes us act. Joy gives us momentum to forge, head first, into whatever task is at hand, happily and optimistically. Joy makes us want to immerse ourselves and stop holding back or protecting ourselves with aloofness or cynicism. For that reason, it is an extremely useful emotion – it gives us confidence, and in our confidence we are open to learning and discovery.

The most important thing when writing with positive emotions is that the emotions authentically chime with you.

Children show a lot of joy – they throw themselves at life with wild abandon and few apprehensions. If you have ever looked at a child and thought, "Life was simpler then" or "Why am I not so eager about the world now?", then writing with joy may be the antidote you need. If you are thinking, "Well, it is easy for kids in the blissful naivety of youth", then you have a point. Cynicism can be protective, and that's why we develop it as we mature, but it can also be damaging. It can close us to new relationships, novel opportunities or life paths that might be just what we need – but we feel too scared to take the risk. Simply put: if you would like to build your confidence, first build up your sense of joy about the world.

A STORY OF WRITING JOY

Valerie was one of several people in The Positive Journalling Study to select joy as an emotion to write with, yet her case study is a particularly interesting one. Valerie is a poet – so writing is how she earns her bread and butter – but even she found there were things to learn from this novel way of writing.

Valerie told me that when writing about her worries or anxieties, she had felt she was "taken" to those negative places, yet writing with positive emotions such as joy helped, instead, to recreate those joyful feelings.

When she wrote with joy, among other positive emotions, Valerie summarized three specific elements that she felt were beneficial about writing this way as opposed to her typical journal writing. First was the mindful, focused element: "You are taking 15 minutes or half an hour to do this," she explained, "so you are not doing anything else... your mind is focused on that one thing." Second, she mentioned positive journalling as a way of "capturing" or "framing" the day in a certain way – almost, you might say, like taking a photo of the day, in its best light. Finally, she added, "You are also recreating whatever it is that you are writing about, so if it is something pleasurable you are getting those pleasurable feelings again."

CASE STUDY

Valerie

Valerie described how she kept coming back to the word *joy* in her positive journal. Each and every paragraph came to be, in one way or another, about this emotion. It made her feel unburdened and free, lighthearted. She said she felt *anchored* by it, like a centripetal force that helped to draw her writing together. This made her feel that the writing had coherence. In one sense, she explained, positive journalling was an extra task in her day, but she also found it was a way to *see the day through joy* – making it an enjoyable tool for reframing the events of the day. This was really beneficial, she said. The positive emotions, such as joy, offered Valerie a kind of window through which to evaluate her day and this felt satisfying.

TAKEAWAY LESSONS

1

WE CAN BE ANCHORED BY POSITIVE EMOTIONS.

Writing in a free-form way is wonderful, but just like being accompanied by a kindly Sherpa on a Himalayan trail, words – particularly positive-emotion words – can be reassuring and welcome guides. Positive emotions can offer us an idea or focus that allows our writing to become more intentional and meditative. Rather than become lost in worry, using positive emotions in our writing can offer a torch to light our path.

2

WRITING POSITIVELY HELPS US POSITIVELY ASSESS THE DAY.

Even if things have gone wrong, almost invariably there will be some chink of light or hope in the stormiest day. Whether writing with joy or another emotion, this kind of writing helps us to frame the day however we choose, meaning we empower ourselves and are hopefully able to go to bed feeling as though the day has yielded something positive for us.

3

WE CAN RECREATE POSITIVE EMOTIONS IN WRITING.

Researchers have argued that we can recreate or "self-generate" positive emotions. Writing is a tool for doing just this. This could be vital if our circumstances are particularly difficult or there is little we feel we can turn to for a sense of joy. Recalling a joyful time, whether it happened last week or several years ago, can help us to recapture some of those feelings – feelings that are integral to our survival. If this seems like fantasizing, think back to page 18 and the example of the listless cave people: focusing on positive emotions, particularly if our present situations do not necessarily make us feel them, could mean the vital difference between equipping ourselves with the resources to survive and thrive in such circumstances, and leaving us feeling helpless and adrift. This is not about being superficially chirpy; it is about calling on our built-in resources for support.

TEN WAYS TO WRITE WITH JOY

Now that we have explored a little bit of the psychology of joy and looked at a real-life story of writing joy, as well as some key takeaway lessons, let us get more specific: how can *you* use joy in your own writing? Here are some exercises that you might want to try to bring more joy into your journal practice.

Remember, in every exercise, to be *detailed and descriptive* – the more you engage all of your senses when writing with an emotion such as joy, the more your sense of joy will potentially be stimulated. If you are writing about the joy of quiet mornings, then write about sipping hot coffee, the shafts of light through the blinds, the smooth feel of floorboards under bare feet, the homely aroma and crunch of warm toast... Grab a pen, some paper and a quiet moment or two, and get started.

one

WRITE ABOUT A TIME IN THE PAST THAT BROUGHT YOU JOY. Maybe it was one of those perfect days in your childhood, at the seaside or a long summer afternoon in the garden. What happened? Where were you? What were you feeling besides joy? How might this joyous time make you feel about other areas of your life?

two

WRITE ABOUT A FUTURE TIME THAT YOU ANTICIPATE WILL BRING JOY. Find something to look forward to, whether it is a visit to or from a loved one, the fresh scent of a new season or even just a coffee date with a good friend. What do you expect to happen? What are you most looking forward to about it?

three

FIND JOY IN THE PRESENT MOMENT. We are often looking behind or ahead of ourselves, and rarely at what is happening right now. We forget the everyday joys because we take them for granted. Think of the joy of cosy socks or of being in good health, or the simple joy of your partner bringing you a cup of tea – these things do not get old, we just forget to take note of them. Sharpen your senses to the minute wonders that make up your everyday world.

four

WRITE ABOUT A PERSON WHO BRINGS YOU PARTICULAR JOY. This could be a partner or loved one, or an artist, musician or author you particularly like and whose work makes you joyous. Write about how and why you associate them with your joy, or how they embody joy.

five

WRITE ABOUT WHAT JOY FEELS LIKE, LOOKS LIKE, TASTES LIKE OR SMELLS LIKE. What colour would joy be if it had one? What kind of scent would it have? This may seem trite, but in fact we often think and speak in metaphor ("I feel blue today" or "I smell a rat"), so thinking of new metaphors can help us feel entirely differently about, or more in touch with, a given emotion.

six

WRITE ABOUT HOW YOU COULD THINK OF JOY DIFFERENTLY. We have all heard the phrase "limiting beliefs" bandied about but, as with many common clichés, there is truth in this one. If you believe that joy can only be rainbow birthday cake and sand between your toes on a sunny isle, and you do not have these things, then you are limiting your experience of this emotion. Birthday cake and sunny holidays are great, but so are cool wintery walks to work and a nutritious homemade packed lunch, in their own way. Focus in on how joy can be found in unexpected places, and write about that.

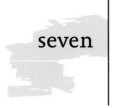

seven

WRITE ABOUT HOW YOU BRING JOY TO OTHERS, OR HOW YOU MIGHT AIM TO. Joy is not just about us – most of the joyous occasions you can recall almost certainly involved others: those big belly laughs with friends at the cinema, or a family wedding day or other affection-filled event. Sometimes the present-*giving* of Christmas Day really is more heart-warming than the receiving. Just as when a friend is afraid and the fear rubs off on us, joy is contagious, too. Write about spreading joy around, and you might find it comes back to you.

eight

WRITE ABOUT HOW YOU COULD BEGIN A DAILY PRACTICE OF JOY. How could you infuse every single day with a little burst of joy, however small? Think of two typical scenarios that help joy emerge: surprise and other people. Maybe you could make a habit of regularly changing your phone's background to photos of fun with friends – joy and connection in one! Write any other ideas you can think of.

nine

WRITE ABOUT FINDING JOY IN YOUR SURROUNDINGS.
One thing that binds almost all of us is habitat – we
all have one (our home, city or country) and we all
ultimately share one (the planet). Too often, we ignore
our surroundings; we conceptualize "us" and "the
environment", not realizing that this – *all of this!* – is
the environment. We are in it. Write about the bits of
the world that facilitate your joy, from the interesting
architecture of a gallery to quiet blue skies or the kind of
drenching rain that romantic comedy is founded on.

ten

WRITE ABOUT JOY AS CONFIDENCE. This chapter has looked at
how intertwined feeling joy is with feeling confident, so why not
try writing in a way that brings the two together: how do you
associate joy and confidence? What would a joyful person who
entered the room now look like? What would a confident person
look like? Are they similar? Write a description of this, and any
insights you can take away from it.

Writing Gratitude

Writing can sometimes feel like breathing: necessary, sustaining, a way of keeping ourselves alive. Sometimes words are little gasps of surprise. Sometimes sentences are deep sighs of recalibration. Sometimes paragraphs tumble out quickly, like gulps for air. Though, whether urgent or luxuriating, for someone driven to put his or her experience into words, writing can often feel like an essential and automatic response to life – but you do not need to feel this strong, indispensable sense of writing to benefit from it. If you are able, and inclined, to pick up a pen and form words, then you can benefit from writing. The problem is that doing what is good for us does not always come easily (as most of us will have encountered at least once or twice in life!).

Also in this category of good-for-us-but-not-easy is giving thanks. Gratitude is a cornerstone of many of the world's religions for a reason: because it makes us feel fulfilled, connected and brings a sense of purpose. What does this wild life amount to if we do not stop once in a while and say, "That was pretty good, wasn't it?" This, however, does not always happen naturally. We are too busy enjoying things to remember to say thanks for them. Therefore, in the secular world – without the rituals of a religion – we often forget about it altogether.

We read a lot these days about the benefits of gratitude. Gratitude is the kale smoothie of the emotions. Yet, just like green beverages, it is not always that appetizing. Gratitude can feel banal, become forced and even seem like a chore – and if it does, many of its benefits can be lost. Yet gratitude is, as much as anything else, about perspective. Because of this, writing is an excellent tool for dwelling on and developing gratitude – because writing is also a way of *perceiving*. You might like to think of practising gratitude as lifting the tablecloth of any given moment and inspecting the table legs underneath, noting the pillars that support everything you take for granted. What do you see when you lift the tablecloth?

THE PSYCHOLOGY
OF GRATITUDE

Gratitude is a beguiling topic that has provided ample grist for the mills of psychological researchers everywhere, who have found that gratitude significantly increases wellbeing in many ways. In particular, they emphasize the lift in mood it gives us, known to scientists as "positive affect".[18] From this comes the idea of keeping a gratitude journal. For many people this can be a positive and supporting practice, though others may find it a somewhat limiting way in which to write. You might not always feel you have something to be grateful for on a day when you have missed the bus, had an argument with your partner and received bad news from the doctor.

One person in The Positive Journalling Study, Jane, who had kept a gratitude journal as a practice before taking part, explained it well. She said that, although keeping a gratitude journal narrowed what she could write about *only* to being grateful, positive journalling, on the other hand, was a way of writing "about all sorts of different and positive things". She emphasized how nice it was to have the choice of emotions to draw on, and mentioned that specifically being grateful in one's writing could potentially "engender a kind of rebellion or resistance". "Whereas," Jane said, "if you have a choice, there is less likely to be resistance."

Jane makes a fair point: resistance is the last thing you want in a journalling practice. It can be hard enough to find the time to pick up a pen and write in the first place, particularly if circumstances make positive journalling a struggle. It simply depends who you are, and what these individual emotions mean to you. Stay with me, though, and take a quick moment to pen your own interpretation of gratitude, to keep in mind as we move through the rest of this chapter.

The following story shows how very difficult it can be to write positively when the circumstances of life are dire. Yet it also shows how, with gentle inner encouragement, at whatever level feels kind and comfortable, we might bring a little gratitude into our writing, despite what is going on around us.

A STORY OF WRITING GRATITUDE

Amanda was going through a particularly difficult time when she took part in The Positive Journalling Study. Her marriage was ending, she explained, and she often found herself in a dark place emotionally, just as any of us would in that situation.

CASE STUDY

Amanda

Amanda described how, in her normal journal, she would often write on the train to work, watching her innermost anxieties tumble out as quickly as the scenery of parks and suburbs flashed by the window. Amanda struggled at first to engage with positive journalling for this very reason, much more so than some of the other participants. She said that her typical kind of journal writing felt like her "negative comfort zone". The positive emotions, for the most part, did not chime with her, and she found it hard to relate to them. "I just didn't feel I had any of those emotions at that time," she said. "Gratitude was the easiest," she continued. "It was the only one I felt I could write about at that point." Amanda mentioned that she wrote gratefully about "friends and connections with friends", as well as the fact that she had work. She seemed surprised when she told me, "I even said something positive about my marriage at the end." Although accessing some of these emotions was difficult for Amanda, looking back on her positive journal did feel good, she said, and she sensed that it was helpful. "I think it is taking me out of my negative comfort zone," she explained, "which is just to write negative things down. It is sort of making me think of good things in my life."

Sometimes, negativity does feel comfortable. For Amanda, daily scribbling on the train had become habitually negative and was her form of security. Of course, if we have been sorely disappointed and hurt by the world, it can feel like a great risk to be optimistic. Optimism often spells vulnerability. What if we are let down again? What if it brings more of this same unbearable grief? For this reason, we stay warmly wrapped in our own hopelessness, and no one who has been through the same would expect otherwise from us.

You might think gratitude would be the last emotion Amanda would want to choose to write with, yet she did. As a result, she found several important, positive aspects of her life that were sustaining her, including good friends and her work. She emphasized that she was not able to truly feel any of the other emotions on offer – that none of them "chimed" with her on that particular day, and that she could not "get in touch" with or "engage" with those emotions. This reinforces the important takeaway that we met in the previous chapter: positive emotions need to genuinely chime with us, otherwise we simply will not benefit from this type of writing and may well feel worse off.

It is sometimes incredibly difficult to engage with certain positive emotions, so if we limit our view of positivity to one or two specific emotions we will only benefit to a limited degree. That is exactly why this book is about engaging with the whole spectrum of our positivity when we write. Gratitude may sometimes be a tricky emotion to feel if we are facing tough times – and it can engender rebellion, as Jane pointed out. Yet that was not the case for Amanda: despite her difficult circumstances, it was the emotion she most readily embraced. This goes to show how very different and unique we all are in terms of our emotions. Like intricately patterned kaleidoscopes, each individual is an elaborate mix of emotions of varying shapes and hues, constantly in motion.

Amanda went on to say that, although she had found it hard to relate to many of the positive emotions in the moment of writing, when she looked back at what she had written she still felt that it was beneficial. She had not felt an immediate lift in mood from the writing – which would be a lot to expect considering her circumstances – but with hindsight she felt it had been a good thing to do. With some time and patience, it seemed that Amanda came to the view that there were "good things" in her life that deserved her recognition, despite the very pressing challenges she faced. This is probably true for most of us. Sometimes compassionate patience with ourselves may be all it takes to see the positive in our experience.

Sometimes compassionate patience with ourselves may be all it takes to see the positive in our experience.

Amanda's story highlights just how difficult it can be to feel a sense of positivity when things are crumbling all around us. It is easy to feel positive when we are experiencing happy circumstances, and harder – but perhaps more needed than ever – when things are tough. Amanda shows us how our individual emotional struggles are things to be accepted, never forced away or repressed. The "negative comfort zone" can be protective in the short term. We must never allow someone to tell us that we *should* be positive – to "cheer up" or "get over it" on a timescale that suits them. Rather, we should choose to explore positivity on our own terms, at our own pace and for our own reasons.

This being said – if and when we feel ready, kindly reassuring ourselves with positive writing often utterly changes our perspective, and therefore might just offer a path out of the "negative comfort zone". This was something Amanda said when talking about writing with positive emotions such as gratitude: that she "had to be more thoughtful" in the writing process. Being more thoughtful about how we interpret the events of our lives can often lead to transformative shifts in these interpretations.

TAKEAWAY LESSONS

1

DO NOT FEEL THE NEED TO *FORCE* ANY OF THESE EMOTIONS IN YOUR WRITING.

Seek the chime of connection with a positive emotion, and begin there. There is a subtle line between gently encouraging ourselves to do something that is likely to be good for us and anxiously coercing ourselves because we think we must. Remember: feeling positive is never mandatory, but is always a possibility. Feel all your feelings: the comfortable and the uncomfortable ones. Go toward those that you sense will serve you best.

2

IF FEELING A CERTAIN EMOTION IS DIFFICULT, JUST HAVE PATIENCE.

If you are gentle with yourself and exercise compassionate patience, you will probably find you can feel any positive emotion – eventually. Positive emotions are context-specific, and the individual contexts of our lives are usually changing all the time. Keep coming tentatively back to positivity, instead of being put off and thinking, "That fluffy stuff is not for me!" Use your writing as a metaphorical thermometer: write with different positive emotions, and check how you warm toward them. If it does not happen right away, try it another day.

3

WRITING WITH A POSITIVE EMOTION CAN BE MORE THOUGHTFUL.

Apart from anything else, writing with a given positive emotion helps us to focus our busy and fretful minds in the writing process. This more mindful approach may even offer us a way out of the negative comfort zone, which can be so tempting in writing. Writing with positive emotions can encourage us to slow down and can prevent us from going on autopilot and regurgitating our most time-honoured gripes, rather than interrogating new possibilities for ourselves.

TEN WAYS TO WRITE WITH **GRATITUDE**

Hopefully this chapter has convinced you that writing your gratitude, when it feels comfortable, is a good idea. Now for a few tips on exactly how you might want to go about trying it for yourself. You will find some specific exercises, but remember that creativity and autonomy are warmly encouraged when it comes to any kind of expressive writing, including positive journalling. You might want to combine one or more exercises, adapt an exercise or go entirely off piste and make up your own from scratch. Whatever works for you.

Just as you did with the exercises from the last chapter, aim to be as detailed and descriptive as possible in your writing. There are so many rich and interesting ways to do this with an emotion such as gratitude; hopefully the description of each exercise will spark your imagination.

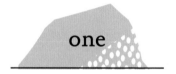

one

WRITE ABOUT A TIME IN THE PAST THAT YOU ARE GRATEFUL FOR. Maybe somebody once put their faith in you, or took a chance on an idea you had, which has affected your present life for the better – a school teacher, an old boss or a relative. Perhaps you might want to write your gratitude for being here in the world at all; for the midwife who delivered you into the world, or for the parent or guardian who offered the attentive care that meant you survived your early years.

two

WRITE ABOUT A FUTURE TIME WHEN YOU ANTICIPATE YOU WILL FEEL GRATITUDE. This may feel unusual, because gratitude is something of a retrospective emotion, and we never really know how things are going to turn out for us. Yet this exercise is not about attempting to control what will happen next in your life, but rather about projecting your gratitude forward to a future point at which you will meet it. Write about the gratitude you might feel when you have passed through a current challenge. Write of your gratitude for what will hopefully be a long life well lived. Or take a shorter-term perspective and simply write about what you are looking gratefully forward to tomorrow.

three

WRITE ABOUT YOUR GRATITUDE FOR THE PRESENT MOMENT. Have you got sustaining work, good health, a cosy home? These are things we often overlook until we lose them; expressing your gratitude in writing can curb this tendency. Is the boiler whirring in the background, keeping you warm? Is your other half in bed beside you, sharing a moment of quiet reading before sleep? Take stock of your immediate situation and excavate it for things to be grateful for.

four

**WRITE ABOUT A PERSON WHO MAKES YOU
PARTICULARLY GRATEFUL.** Do not just write "my
friends are great" – be detailed. Write "Chris always
lends a listening ear, and I have needed that lately"
or "Suzy's laugh is infectious – she always makes me
forget what I was worrying about when we go for
after-work drinks!" Think about perhaps sharing
what you have written with the person. Gratitude
letters, when shared, have been shown to offer
distinct boosts for the wellbeing of all involved.

five

**WRITE ABOUT WHAT GRATITUDE FEELS
LIKE, LOOKS LIKE, TASTES LIKE OR
SMELLS LIKE.** Writing about gratitude
in a novel and descriptive way using our
various senses can help bring the emotion
alive for us in new ways. Does gratitude
have a fresh minty scent, or a mellower
aroma, like burning incense? Is it soft and
satiny like a rabbit's ear, or does it have an
aged grain like antique rosewood? What
flavour would gratitude have? This is a
particularly fertile exercise where your
imagination can run away with you. Let it.

six

WRITE ABOUT HOW YOU COULD THINK OF GRATITUDE DIFFERENTLY. For example, it might not always be about just saying thanks or even feeling thankful – it might be *doing* thankfulness. Write about behaviours that express thankfulness: grateful acts. You might also think of gratitude in terms of some further metaphors, and write about that. Is your gratitude a deep-rooted oak or a buzzing meadow awash with blooming wildflowers? Are there any other ways you might think of gratitude differently?

seven

WRITE ABOUT WHAT OTHERS MIGHT BE GRATEFUL FOR IN YOU. It is important that this exercise does not become expectant – that you don't begin to feel people *should* express their gratitude for what you offer them. Other people's gratitude is not something you can control, so it would be futile to assume otherwise. Instead, focus on what you give freely and unconditionally, without any expectation of thanks or appreciation, like milk to a baby or a warm hug to a grieving friend.

eight

WRITE ABOUT HOW YOU COULD BEGIN A DAILY PRACTICE OF GRATITUDE. As this chapter has already stressed, starting a daily practice of gratitude should be handled with care. Less is sometimes more with this emotion, and it can definitely "wear out" as a practice. But there is nothing to stop you experimenting in your own life. Would some kind of regular practice of gratitude suit you? If so, how might you begin this? Write out some different options that seem appealing. You might try a prayer of thanks at the end of the day, either spiritual or secular. Or you might opt for a word of thanks to your partner each morning, or ten minutes of meditating on gratitude before you leave the house for work.

nine

WRITE ABOUT FEELING GRATITUDE FOR YOUR SURROUNDINGS.
Writing is often an indoor activity, but when we break this routine (and weather permits!) writing outdoors can give a refreshing boost to our practice. Even if you cannot get outside to write, you can allow the writing itself be an exploration of the great outdoors. Write about the wonders of the natural world that you are grateful for – there are a lot to choose from. The salt spray of a roaring ocean. The hidden birds twittering along a dappled woodland path. That hour of twilight when a slight chill sets in and the air becomes suddenly crisp and electric with the coming of the night. What are you most grateful for in nature?

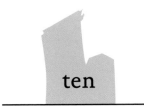

ten

WRITE ABOUT GRATITUDE AS CONNECTION.
The emotion of gratitude is often specifically tied up with our connection to others. When we feel thankful, typically what we are thankful for is the hard work or care of the people around us. Expressing gratitude for these individuals and groups can help us to feel closer to them. Could gratitude bring you closer to your colleagues? Your partner? Your siblings, children or parents? Perhaps even a stranger? Explore this in your writing.

Writing
Serenity

Writing takes time. Quiet minutes and hours slipping by on the clock face to only the meditative scratch of our pen on paper, or our fingers clicking computer keys. Things that take time – well, they often involve some measure of procrastination. At the end of his TED talk, "Inside the Mind of a Master Procrastinator", Tim Urban shares a slide he calls a Life Calendar. It is simply a series of small boxes, one for every week of a 90-year life. The number of boxes – and more specifically how very few they seem – is somewhat alarming. With so little time to waste, so many pressures to make these weeks count – including making sure we are taken care of in every box, and that others we love are taken care of – we can begin to view anything that takes a significant chunk of our time with suspicion. Serenity, then, is one of the emotions we are least set up to experience in contemporary Western life.

That is why it is so necessary.

The *Oxford Dictionary of English* describes serenity as "the state of being calm, peaceful and untroubled". How often are you in that state? Are you *ever* in that state? Between the alarm going off, work getting done, the washing going on, the dinner being cooked and falling back into bed at a reasonable hour, few of us can call serenity a major feature of our life.

Mindfulness and mindfulness meditation have surged in popularity in recent years. You may have even tried it yourself. Yet there is another way to bring a practice of peace and calm into our lives: journalling.

THE PSYCHOLOGY
OF SERENITY

Calmness can often feel elusive in modern life. Stress, by its very nature, does not leave us time to ponder how calm we feel, or even to contemplate whether or not feeling calm is important. Stress averts our gaze. Stress keeps us distracted, and for this reason stress can, sometimes quite by surprise, become chronic. This makes feeling serenity tricky, because we tend to experience it when we are feeling comfortable or at ease – not running around, flustered and preoccupied! Psychologically speaking, moments of serenity make us feel "at one" with our given situation or set of surroundings. Serenity arises out of our contentment and calm satisfaction with things *just as they are*.[19]

When we use the word serenity, what we often mean is a sense of peace. Finding inner peace is at the heart of many of the great Eastern philosophies and is something we Westerners have developed quite a thirst for, given our hectic and overwrought style of living. In his book *The Positive Psychology of Buddhism and Yoga*, research psychologist Marvin Levine illuminates many useful ways in which we can think about serenity. He offers as an example the extraordinary equanimity of His Holiness the Dalai Lama. A pillar of serenity, the Dalai Lama once responded to a television reporter (who was querying whether or not he feels resentment towards the Chinese for their influence in Tibet) that it was one thing for the Chinese to have stolen his country, yet quite another to allow them to *steal his mind*.[20]

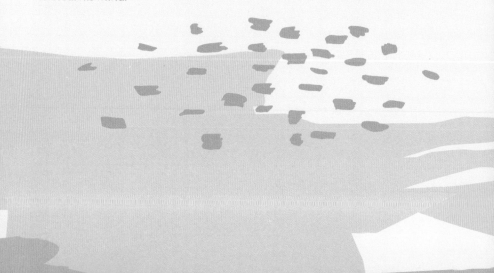

What is "stealing" your mind at the moment? Work? A goal you have failed to reach? A fall-out with a friend or loved one? Serenity, as the Dalai Lama so poignantly puts it, is about not allowing someone – or something – to steal your inner sense of peace. This, of course, is easier said than done. We all exist in the hustle-bustle of the real world, and maintaining serenity amid all this can be a challenge to say the least. Yet, it is possible.

What we should be careful of, however, is allowing the "pursuit" of serenity to be itself an added stress to us. If what our minds are suffering is stress, then by desperately chasing serenity – and having the frustrating sense that we are "failing" in this pursuit – we have rather missed the point and have just lumped an extra stress on ourselves. We cannot chase serenity and grab it by the coat tails. Rather, if we wait quietly enough, serenity might just come and perch on our shoulder like a shy little bird.

With this in mind, take a moment now to reflect on your own individual interpretation of serenity.

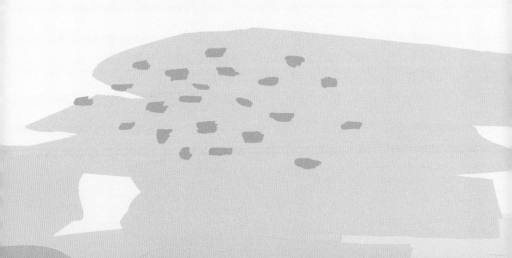

A STORY OF WRITING SERENITY

When Louise took part in The Positive Journalling Study, her father was terminally ill. Yet, even in such dark times, she was willing to sit and try writing with positive emotions. This shows the remarkable human capacity for resilience and optimism amid our suffering.

CASE STUDY

Louise

Louise chose to write with serenity because she felt it was something that she strongly needed in her life. She revealed that, although serenity had felt necessary that day, it had not been easy. She had not had what she felt was a serene day – though, she emphasized, a serene day is different things to different people. So many of her days had not been serene, she said, in part because of the great difficulty she was facing in her father being ill. But, despite this, in her writing she was able to note things that did bring a sense of serenity. A simple walk in the park had been a highlight. Spending time alone in her bedroom writing in her journal itself became a serene act. Louise described her positive journalling as a way of looking after herself, almost as though she were "dipping herself in kindness". The act of writing helped her to realize how important serenity was to her each day, even on those days that did not feel particularly serene.

In positive journalling we do not necessarily have to write about the emotion we are feeling at that moment.

Louise's experience of writing serenity shows that in positive journalling we do not necessarily have to write about the emotion we are feeling at that moment. We do not even have to choose an emotion that we think we are *able* to feel at that moment. We can simply write about what we know we need. When a good friend wants to look after us in a difficult time, they will often console us by saying, "You will be fine, it will be okay," even though they probably realize we are unable to see this truth – they know it is what we need, and they will offer it up in various guises until we are ready to see it ourselves. In this sense, writing can be a way of looking after ourselves. Next time you turn to your journal, ask yourself, "How can I look after myself in my writing today?"

All of the positive writing prompts in this book offer an enjoyable new way of looking at writing, but this is particularly true in the case of writing serenity – because so many of us are starved of this emotion. As we have seen, modern Western life is particularly badly suited to experiences of serenity and for that reason, just like Louise, we must give it to ourselves as a purposeful gift.

Louise's account shows that serenity, like the act of journal writing itself, tends to be solitary. Importantly, this does not mean it is selfish – at least not in the negative sense of that word. Yes, taking quiet time just to sit or write can be very focused on the self – especially when, as we have seen, the writing becomes purely fretful and we find ourselves stuck in our "negative comfort zone". If this happens, then we often find we *stay* self-focused (think repetitive, woe-is-me-type writing). The wonderful thing about positive emotions, however, is that they tend to move our focus *away* from ourselves. Positive emotions actively connect us to others. This is either explicit (we feel love for a spouse, pride in a child and so on), or simply that these emotions are a means of opening us to potential connection because they soften our defences.

Positive emotions relax our tightly wound egos and open us up to the possibility of relating to others. When a colleague has lost all hope in a project, it is tricky to get them to listen and communicate with you, because their doubt has closed them down. If a partner has stopped feeling love toward you, it can be impossible to connect with them, however hard you try. If we ourselves lose joy in an activity, we quickly get turned off and our attention shuts down or wanders. Clearly, in the absence of positive emotion, we shrivel, we retreat and we close up as flowers do as the sun fades to night. Often this "closing off" is necessary and protective – we do not want to leave ourselves wide open to potential outside threats. Yet, when being closed becomes habitual, it can hinder us and be corrosive. Therefore, adding an intentional practice of positive emotion to our lives, as we do with a positive journal, is far from selfish: journalling this way supports our connections with others. Of course, this is easier some days than others.

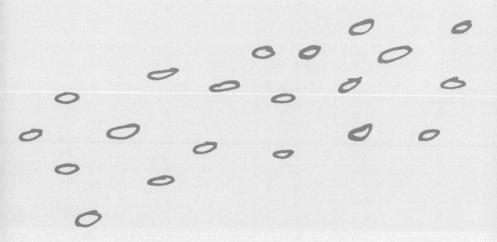

When Louise observed that a serene day means different things to different people, she was exactly right. Serenity, like most of our emotions, is context-specific. This is a useful thing to keep in mind when working through this book. There may be points at which you say, "Hang on a minute – I really do not agree with that." In those moments, do one thing and one thing only: ignore the book entirely. Go with your gut. I am encouraging you to do this because struggling to get on board with an interpretation that plainly does not sit right with you is a sure-fire way to get fed up with the whole endeavour of writing positively. We do not all have to agree on our definitions of different positive emotions or what they feel like. Positive journalling ought to feel profoundly fulfilling for you, and the surest way of dampening this is to shoehorn yourself into a description that does not fit. The surest way of achieving it is to write with sincerity and authenticity.

TAKEAWAY LESSONS

1

WE CAN WRITE WHAT WE NEED, NOT WHAT WE FEEL.

Writing will never be a magic balm that instantly gives us the feeling we are hungering for, but it does allow us at least to make that need plain and to begin the steps toward it. This is not about exhaustive striving, but announcing what we need. It may be that after one or even several journalling sessions on a certain emotion you still do not feel you have "tapped into" it. Nevertheless, the simple act of noting what is needed is a profound step in any journey to a happier life – as long as we can face that need compassionately and non-judgementally.

2

EXPLORING POSITIVE EMOTIONS, SUCH AS SERENITY, IN A WRITING PRACTICE IS NOT SELFISH

Rather, these emotions open us to the possibility of deeper connection with others. If we can learn to self-generate these emotions, to whatever degree and within any practice – whether this is positive journalling or another approach such as loving-kindness meditation – we will probably see great benefits to our relationships. One reason for this is that taking the time to support ourselves in our journal often means we can be a better support to others. Think about it: if we feel calm and serene after journalling, we then have this serenity to offer others.

3 WE DO NOT ALL HAVE TO AGREE ON POSITIVE EMOTIONS.

Serenity may have entirely different connotations for you from what it has for me. That is okay. What matters most in this kind of practice is bringing a genuine sincerity to your writing. This being said, we must all be open to recognizing that our notions of a positive emotion may benefit from evolution and modification. This is a process that can easily be spurred when we take a closer look at these emotions and examine definitions we may have simply inherited or taken for granted. Journalling is an excellent way to interrogate these inherited definitions.

TEN WAYS TO WRITE WITH **SERENITY**

This set of writing exercises will be a little different from the ones offered in the previous chapters. In those chapters I emphasized the importance of projecting your mind both forward and backward in time, to mine your life for experiences of particular emotions and reap the fruit once again. There is less of that focus here – although there is some – because serenity is usually to be found by making peace with the present moment. Another important aspect to writing serenity that you may want to try is to *set up your space*. This could be true of any kind of positive journalling, but here it is particularly effective. If you are aiming to offer yourself the emotion of serenity, this will only be helped by setting up a relaxed and grounding space – settling you into the activity, into listening to your inner world and noticing your sensations.

You may choose to spread out a blanket at the quiet end of the garden, where you can sit peacefully, uninterrupted. Perhaps you will light a candle, or simply shut the door to the bedroom, as Louise did. Maybe it is a dark, chilly morning and you want to swaddle yourself in your bedcovers and write by lamplight. Do whatever it takes to make you feel that you are taking a little break from the furore of the world. Then write.

one

MAKE A STATEMENT ABOUT WHY YOU
NEED SERENITY, AND BE A WITNESS
TO THAT NEED. Serenity is not about
forgoing or repressing your strife: it is
about going right into it so that you
can go through it. Making a statement
about precisely what you are suffering
under, not only as a vent but also as
a statement of intent, is a powerful
way to begin this process. You may
find yourself wanting to go into great
detail – and if so you should welcome
this – but do try not to get lost here.
Recall the image from the chapter on
writing joy, of the emotion being your
anchor, steadily drawing you back
even as you allow yourself to wander
into darker places.

two

WRITE ABOUT GIVING YOURSELF
SERENITY AS A GIFT. This is a good
exercise to follow on with after stating
why you need serenity. Now you are
stating how you will begin to offer it
to yourself. It might be nice to write
this through the metaphor of a literal
gift. Visualize serenity as a beautifully
wrapped box that you are handing
to yourself. You might even want to
write some dialogue between these
two inner selves: the giver and the
receiver. Say "Thank you" to yourself.
Say "You are welcome" in return. Write
whatever else arises when you place
these two facets of your psyche in
conversation.

three

FIND SERENITY IN THE PRESENT MOMENT. Even if your mind feels scattered and your thoughts fraught, what *do* you feel serene about right now? This may seem an odd question and you might instinctively think, "I am suffering! There is nothing serene about this scenario!" Yet allow yourself to look beyond that suffering, even just momentarily, to the unnoticed elements of the present moment. Are you physically comfortable – in a warm home or soft chair? Find serenity there. Are you physically well, with no pressing pains or discomfort? Find serenity there. Write this as a kind of hide and seek: where is serenity hiding, underneath your suffering? Keep exploring deeper, beyond the obvious.

four

WRITE ABOUT A PERSON WHO EPITOMIZES SERENITY FOR YOU OR WHO MAKES YOU FEEL SERENE. Is there someone in your life who always swoops in and takes the stress out of any situation? Does a particular friend carry calmness into a room simply by being there? Write about this person in some detail. What is at the root of their serenity or at the root of your feeling serene around them? Write about how you might channel this, even when they are not around.

five

WRITE ABOUT WHAT SERENITY FEELS LIKE, LOOKS LIKE, TASTES LIKE OR SMELLS LIKE. This exercise will be familiar now from the previous chapters. Employ all of your senses to begin thinking of serenity in more metaphorical terms. Is serenity soft and comforting like an eiderdown, or crisp like linen? Would serenity taste like cool cucumber water or hot, sweet mint tea? Might it have the scent of rain on warm stone or the fragrance of a breeze through pine trees?

six

WRITE ABOUT HOW YOU COULD THINK OF SERENITY DIFFERENTLY. This is a useful activity to allow you to access serenity even in circumstances that feel fraught. Think of it as "sneaking through the back door" of serenity. Is serenity about facing life calmly but head on, or is it about retreating into bed with your laptop for several hours of your favourite TV show, until you are ready to face the world again? Does serenity have to mean an hour of meditation, or could it be a few seconds of deep breathing as the kettle boils? Look for definitions of serenity that are opposed to your previously held ideas. This is a way of inviting serenity into your life even if you don't imagine your present situation is perfectly favourable for it.

seven

WRITE ABOUT HOW YOU BRING SERENITY TO OTHERS. Even if you are a busy or even an anxious person, your presence probably makes at least one person feel calmer or reassured, whether it is a child or other relative, or your boss, who is eased by your taking tasks off his or her hands. Perhaps it is your cat, snoozing comfortably in your lap! Our presence often reassures others so that they can give a sigh of relief. Write about how you might turn this in on yourself, to offer yourself reassurance.

eight

WRITE ABOUT HOW YOU COULD BEGIN, OR DEVELOP, A DAILY PRACTICE OF SERENITY. Again, it is important not to allow this to become a stressful pursuit in itself and miss the point altogether. Do not write goals set in stone, but simply ideas that you might like to test out to see if any "stick". Did you know that green spaces have been shown to promote our mental wellbeing?[21] Find five minutes of your lunch break to be near some grass or trees. Make a habit of mindfully enjoying your morning shower with your various senses, and write about all the little details. What does hot water feel like? What does the pressure of the spray on your back sound like? What does your soap or shower cream smell of? Writing this way can help you to pay due attention to the minutiae of these moments, and centre your focus on the now.

nine

WRITE ABOUT FINDING SERENITY IN YOUR SURROUNDINGS. I have mentioned green spaces, but there are so many other places – even entirely unexpected places – to find serenity. Maybe the passing scenery of your train journey brings you a sense of calm. Maybe there is a café you particularly like because of its cosy chairs and quiet atmosphere. Maybe your bedroom is a shrine of tranquillity. Write about these different surroundings in detail. You may feel you want to recall a serene place from your past, perhaps a relaxed holiday by the sea, or simply imagine a serene environment, like sitting at the foot of a large oak tree, leaning against it for support.

ten

WRITE ABOUT SERENITY AS SELF-KNOWLEDGE. Psychologists have shown that serenity can help us to cultivate a more complex understanding of who we are, and to become more aware of our priorities.[22] You might like to think of this as self-knowledge. What does the quiet contemplativeness of serenity help you to realize about yourself? What emerges when you take yourself away from life's hectic pace and sit with yourself in kind silence? Explore this in detail on the page.

Writing
Interest

Writing is about change. It is about changing experience into words, changing our course on the page and, perhaps, even changing ourselves along that course. Some of us are particularly interested in change, and some of us are not. Even if we prefer the conditions of our lives to stay eternally the same, however, there is a certain amount of change that we cannot avoid: seasons, time, ageing and even loss...

We humans, for the most part, find incredible sources of resilience in times of upheaval. But sometimes we flounder. Change alarms us, and quite understandably. When it comes to the recurrent forms of change like the seasons, or bureaucratic changes at work, or changes in our relationships, we equip ourselves much better if we can be curious and intrigued, rather than perturbed and vaguely distraught: in other words, if we take an interest in change. This does not mean passively accepting changes that we might actively impact; rather it is a potential antidote to cynical apathy.

What does it feel like to be interested in something? How does it feel to want to know more, to be drawn to metaphorically bury our noses in something, like a woodland fox snuffling around in fallen leaves? Sometimes interest occurs quite naturally: a game, a person, an activity draws our attention and we want to explore – to uncover its mysteries. Or, sometimes, we choose to take an active interest. We can take a moment to purposefully "think outside the box" – to delve into an unknown topic, perhaps by reading an unfamiliar book, searching the web for information or approaching an expert.

This chapter will look at what psychologists have to say about interest – for example, is interest really an emotion? Then we will explore a story of writing interest. Once again, at the end of the chapter you will find a bundle of – hopefully *interesting* – writing prompts.

THE PSYCHOLOGY OF INTEREST

Psychologists have taken a great deal of interest in interest. One of the biggest questions that they have pondered in recent years is: is interest an emotion? One psychologist, Paul Silvia, has called interest a somewhat eccentric emotion because it is often left out of lists of our "major" emotions and is even rejected as an emotion altogether by some scientists.[23] But Silvia, along with many others, makes a compelling case for viewing interest as an emotion. He invites us to think of it as one of our *knowledge emotions* – a category that includes other, similarly intellectual emotions, such as confusion and surprise. Take a moment now to think about how you experience this emotion.

We tend to feel interest in situations where we sense that we are safe, but that also provide us with some novelty. We become interested by challenges or mysteries we encounter, that draw our attention but do not overwhelm us – instead, they give us the desire to explore, learn and ultimately expand ourselves.[24] For these reasons, interest is a great motivator. If a movie trailer, for example, does not fundamentally interest us, then it is unlikely we will be motivated to go to the cinema. The big movie bosses know that, which is why trailers have become increasingly loud, brash and fast-paced: they cannot risk losing our attention even for a moment or they know they have lost us forever.

Interest also has a role to play in environments where we learn. A dull topic at school when you were a child would probably have had your eyes wandering to the window and your mind daydreaming, but a fun activity – such as a messy painting session – probably had your eyes glued to the venture. Interest motivates us to learn for its own sake, and because of this it is an emotion that inspires us to develop new skills, knowledge and life experience. Interest helps us both to survive and to thrive.

In the chapter "Putting Positive Psychology into Practice" (pages 37–55), we looked at how emotions move and stir us, either toward or away from certain people, places and activities. This is particularly true of interest. It is an emotion that pushes us toward new things. The power of interest to motivate us to encounter novelty, to discover and learn is a beautiful aspect of most lives, and something that many of us would do well to cultivate. In fact, most psychologists agree that having motivation to encounter new things is essential for living well. Imagine if, as a child, you had not been intrigued to learn how things in the world worked. Or, as a teenager, you had had no interest in befriending others. Such a lack of interest makes life stagnant and lonely. It means forging far fewer relationships with others, learning very little and, as a result, *growing very little* in our lives.

All this makes a pretty strong case for interest as an emotion. So how might we begin to think about writing interest?

A STORY OF
WRITING INTEREST

Laura decided to take part in The Positive Journalling Study because she
was a regular journal writer. She also worked as a life coach and enjoyed
being a grandmother.

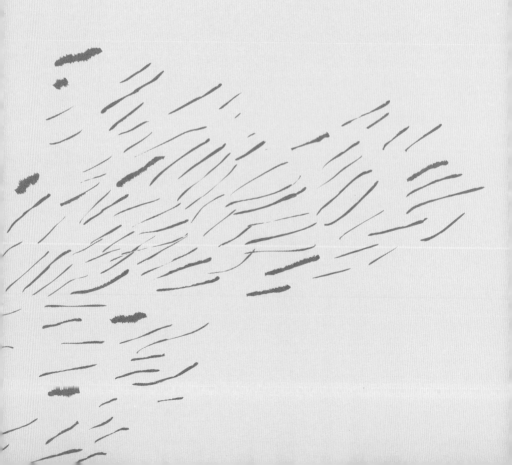

CASE STUDY

Laura

Laura's ordinary way of journalling was ten minutes of "morning pages" every day – a technique recommended by writer Julia Cameron in the book *The Artist's Way*. This practice involves writing two or three pages of unfiltered thoughts and feelings each morning. When Laura was asked about how her emotions typically came into play in this ordinary journal writing, at first she paused. She said this was because she wanted to answer truthfully; then she opened up that she had been suffering with depression. Journalling helped her to find a non-judgemental place to go, and a container for her emotions. When she tried positive journalling, she noted that the structure it offered her, which initially felt like a constraint, soon became a welcomed way to reflect, deeply and honestly, on her life. She was drawn to the emotion of interest, although she said that this was an emotion she rarely noticed in her life. She used interest to write about a special moment with her grandson from that very day. "I'd gone out to see the grandchildren," she began, and then explained how her grandson had approached her. "He showed me some toy that he had been given and I started to play with him... That does not happen very often." Laura described how interested her grandson had been in the toy, so much so that it had captured her interest, and this made her feel they were "both united" in the emotion. "It was very nice," she said. "It was delightful, actually."

A lot of us use a journal as a place to "download" our most challenging and upsetting thoughts. Although this may be extremely helpful, it can also be repetitive. Sometimes we veer into worrisome cycles of thought. In Laura's case, despite this self-confessed tendency to fret, incredibly she felt she was able to "write herself out" of her depression. Perhaps you can relate to Laura's experience. Maybe throughout your life it has been times of distress that have brought you to your journal for support and, just like Laura, you may have found it helpful in making you feel better.

But what if we are not able to "write ourselves out" of depression? This is a tall order, to say the least. What if writing "a lot of negative feelings" simply becomes habitual and perpetual? It may mean that we begin to make an association between our journal and our distress: opening up the pages to see paragraph after paragraph of grief. And this could mean that we gradually find we do not want to be with ourselves there on the page. It is important for us to face our hardships, but inhabiting them over and over again on the page might not always help, and could even be detrimental. As an alternative, what if we began to think of our journal as somewhere we could also, just as habitually, be consciously – and authentically – positive?

When Laura tried writing with positive emotions, she felt a bit "constrained" at first, but quickly came to appreciate the structure and focus it offered her. She explained that this was because her typical journalling-as-usual, in her own words, tended to be quite random. Vitally, having this structure did not limit how reflective or honest Laura felt she could be in the writing, even if it felt constraining at first. She said, "I've re-read those three pages and they really are quite deeply and honestly reflective." Laura's point here echoes Valerie's story on page 63: positive emotions can offer us anchors in our writing. Keeping a journal is much like taking a magnifying glass to whatever is going on in our world. It is up to us, then, to keep a balance between magnifying – or anchoring ourselves to – our melancholy, as opposed to our happiness. Writing should allow us not only to empty our hearts of hardship, but to fill our hearts up with the good.

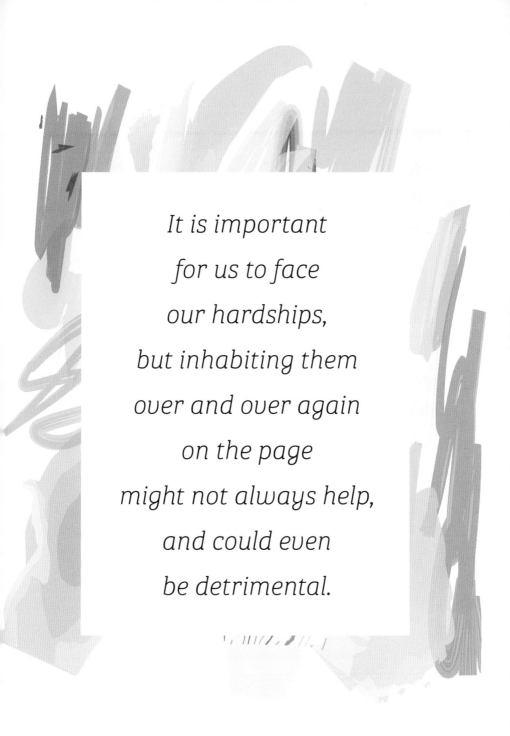

*It is important
for us to face
our hardships,
but inhabiting them
over and over again
on the page
might not always help,
and could even
be detrimental.*

*Exploring interest
is a method for
exploring the spectrum
of our emotions,
including the fleeting,
the elusive and the
easily overlooked.*

Laura explained why she had chosen to write her interest, and how this felt. She said that the emotion stood out to her and that she found herself wondering why it was there. When she began to write she found herself exploring what interest really meant and questioning whether she ever felt truly interested in anything – she realized that she rarely did. She reflected on a sweet moment with her grandson that she felt related to the emotion of interest. Might this moment have been lost for her if she had been using her typical journalling technique? If she had simply been offloading her negative feelings, she would probably not have felt encouraged to look for moments of positive emotion. What a shame this would have been, particularly as we can see in Laura's account how little many of us experience some of these key emotions. It is a pity that we often let these moments slip by, because they are so deeply nourishing to us. They can even "unite" us with others, and are there at our disposal all the time.

This is a vital feature of the practice of positive journalling. It is a method for exploring the whole spectrum of our emotions, including the fleeting, the elusive and the easily overlooked. Journalling in this way is not simply about the stand-out emotions such as angst or even elation. Our emotional life is not a game of pinball, bouncing between extremes: there is subtlety and nuance to it and, although we often feel driven to explore this nuance in our negative emotions, we tend to do this less with the positive. Laura showed that going deeply into our experience of a positive emotion could throw up just as many powerful insights as going into our negative emotions.

TAKEAWAY LESSONS

 1

HABITUALLY WRITING THE NEGATIVE, ALTHOUGH CATHARTIC, MIGHT BECOME DETRIMENTAL.

We often instinctively turn to writing during tough times; when things are going well we might not even think about it. There is nothing inherently wrong with this, but we might want to ask how much it is really serving us. When our writing verges on repetitive worrying, then introducing some positive emotions could serve as something of an antidote. More than this, positive journalling is a kind of savouring. Who says we should not indulge our positive emotions as much as our negative? This may not be instinctive, but think of it as being a bit like exercise. Sometimes we have to take ourselves for a jog because modern life has evolved to have us sitting on our bottoms most of the time. Sometimes we also have to take ourselves deeply into our positive emotions, because modern life has evolved to leave us starved of genuine positivity – leaving us instead with the hollow, canned laughter of our sitcoms and the forced cheer of corporate "team-building" days.

2

POSITIVE JOURNALLING MIGHT FEEL CONSTRAINED – AT FIRST!

If it does, choose to look at writing with specific emotions as a first step to writing in a more free-form, positive way. The concept of positive journalling is, primarily, simply to "round out" the experience of writing in a journal: to give equal precedence to our uncomfortable and our pleasurable emotions. Once we begin to get to know our more positive emotions on the page, in all their nuances, then the "prompt" of a single positive emotion will probably no longer be necessary, but it is a good place to start.

3

POSITIVE EMOTIONS CAN BE FLEETING AND EASILY FORGOTTEN. POSITIVE JOURNALLING HELPS US TO CAPTURE THEM.

Only by writing in detail about her interest did Laura see that it was a potentially very important emotion for her, and one that she linked with bonding to her grandson, even though it was not an emotion that she felt she experienced often. Do not assume you know everything there is to know about your positive emotions. Do not whitewash your positivity with the word "happy" or "cheerful" – instead, take a magnifying glass to the complex tapestry of your positivity, look for surprising little moments where positive emotions arise, and see what you find.

TEN WAYS TO WRITE WITH **INTEREST**

It is time for you to have a go at writing your interest. Remember that these are only prompts and ideas – you are free to go wherever you want with this – but hopefully the exercises will act as a fun, "get started" guide, and will intrigue you.

Using detail and description in our writing is important to cultivating the emotions in this book – but this should never feel dry or laborious. If you are writing about an interesting piece of art, if writing about the intricate detail of the paintwork makes you yawn, instead reflect on the hours of love and attention that the artist would have spent on the piece. Or write about how you felt on seeing it, in your mind and in your body. You could even write about how that feeling affected the rest of your day in a positive way. Wherever detail takes you that feels *interesting*, go there.

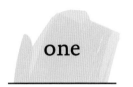

one

WRITE ABOUT A TIME IN THE PAST
THAT WAS INTERESTING. Perhaps
it was reading a brilliant book, or
crafting an essay you had to write on
a topic that was enthralling, or even
a documentary film you watched
that blew your mind. It could be a
particular gallery you visited, or a
museum exhibition that you attended
with a friend. What about it made you
feel interest, and what was that like?
Could you perhaps bring this feeling of
interest into another area of your life?

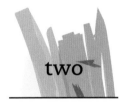

two

WRITE ABOUT A FUTURE TIME
THAT YOU ANTICIPATE WILL BE
INTERESTING. Maybe you have a book
on your shelf that you have been
dying to read and you are just waiting
for a moment of peace this weekend.
Maybe you have a city break coming
up, to somewhere that you have never
been. What do you think will be most
interesting about this? Why do you
think you will find it interesting?

three

***

FIND INTEREST IN THE PRESENT MOMENT. Even if you are sneaking in ten minutes of journalling before work and are sitting at the kitchen table in your dressing gown, it may still be possible to find some point of interest. Take interest in a tree you can see from the window, or how the cat does her exercises in the early sunlight, or even ponder the history of kitchens and how the mod cons of yours would be nothing like anything your great-great-grandparents had. You might even simply want to take interest in your own inner world – an important feature of journalling. What interesting feelings and thoughts within you are currently unfolding? What are you interested in seeing yourself achieve today?

four

WRITE ABOUT A PERSON WHO PARTICULARLY INTERESTS YOU. This could be a public figure, such as a promising new politician, or perhaps a new colleague at work who has some interesting ideas. It might be your own children, grandchildren or a young niece or nephew, and how fast they are growing up and learning about the world. Why are they interesting, and how? Does your interest in them come perhaps from their being very *interested* in the world themselves? Write about this, and think about what you might learn from them.

five

WRITE ABOUT WHAT INTEREST FEELS LIKE, LOOKS LIKE, TASTES LIKE OR SMELLS LIKE. Psychologist Hubert Hermans writes that "metaphor is not to be viewed as an ornament or a mere figure of speech, frequently used by poets or children. On the contrary, metaphor is an indispensable structure of human understanding by which we can figuratively comprehend our world."[25] Have you ever thought, for example, about how "more" is, metaphorically speaking, "up"? Prices go "up", stocks "fall", we turn the heat "down", statistics "rise" – but there is no fixed reason why this should be so. Creating new metaphors in our writing is a way to understand these emotions in a whole new way, to re-access them if they have become dull or commonplace to us. Perhaps interest is cobalt blue and fizzes like electricity. Or perhaps it has the scent of new books. Use your imagination and then write any potential insights, asking yourself why this might be.

six

WRITE ABOUT HOW YOU COULD THINK OF INTEREST DIFFERENTLY. Interest does not, for example, require a mesmerizing revolutionary discovery or intricate details of the next NASA space expedition. The minutiae of our world hold much interest. Think about something as simple as a single blade of grass that has pushed its way up through substantial layers of soil. How that single blade feeds on the sun and how it becomes food to animals; how it is soft and dewy underfoot on a warm spring day, and then crisp and frozen by a winter frost. Find interest in things both great and small.

seven

WRITE ABOUT HOW YOU ARE INTERESTING TO OTHERS. Humans are fascinated by one another – the whole concept of a tabloid newspaper or gossip column is tribute to that. Yet how often do we think about how interesting we are to others? Try to see yourself from another's gaze. What about *you* might be captivating? Do you do interesting work in the world, or have an interesting story to tell? Is your heritage interesting, or is there a particular talent that you have for baking, perhaps, or music? If being overtly positive about yourself is something you struggle with, then think about how what you find interesting might differ from what others find interesting in you. Perhaps people are interested by how quiet you are – a certain air of mystery about you – or even a difficult experience you have had that they might feel empathy with. Challenge your own views of what is interesting in your writing.

eight

WRITE ABOUT HOW YOU COULD BEGIN A DAILY PRACTICE OF INTEREST. We saw in Laura's case that interest can easily become a forgotten emotion. Write some of the things that interest you, and why, then ponder how you might bring more of that into your life. Could you start practising a new language for just 20 minutes a day? Or make the effort to discover a new piece of art each week? Or simply watch a different TED talk each afternoon during your lunch break? Write about how this daily interest might impact other parts of your life.

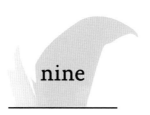

nine

WRITE ABOUT TAKING AN INTEREST IN YOUR SURROUNDINGS. One thing that most of us love about travel is the novelty: suddenly our senses are awash with new buildings, landscapes, colours, scents, flavours... Contrary to this, when we are familiar with a place, it can become humdrum. We go on autopilot and stop being actively interested in it, or even really seeing it. Write about your surroundings with interest: you might begin with the room you are in, the building, the street, the city or even the country. You might want to take this activity to the park or local botanical gardens and try it there. What are the most interesting details? How does taking an interest in your surroundings feel?

ten

WRITE ABOUT INTEREST AS MOTIVATION. On page 117, we looked at how interest and motivation are intricately linked. If you are lacking motivation for a particular activity, think about how you can take a greater interest in it. What does an interested person look like? What does a motivated person look like? Are they the same? Can you learn something from this? Explore these questions in your writing.

Writing
Hope

Writing is a kind of alchemy. We pick through the carbon driftwood of daily experience and, somehow, craft it into luminous treasure. That treasure is words and stories and poetry – and all that they encompass, represent and communicate. This is one reason why writing and hope are such a natural marriage: because hope is a kind of alchemy, too. Hope is a positive emotion, but it typically arises out of difficult times. We do not tend to feel profoundly hopeful unless things have gone wrong or we are yearning for things to improve in some way. We often value hope specifically *because* of difficulty and despair.

How might words evoke hope for you? Well, they probably already have. Who among us has not written a letter, email or diary entry aimed at the object of our unrequited affection? Probably only a lucky few. Those words, if you can recall them, are likely to have been drenched in hopeful longing, doused in the desire for the one you love to be yours and a stirring plea to make them so. Writing such a letter or email probably got you quite worked up. Maybe you shed some tears. Maybe the longing rose to fever-pitch level, so that it became a physical ache. Words did that. Words brought you to that profound physical realization of your emotion. This chapter will show you how to wield this power of words to your advantage – not only to rile and distress you (words definitely do that), but also to encourage, console and inspire you. Importantly, we will look at how this need not necessarily mean going head first into *feeling* the emotion itself. Even in positive journalling, sometimes *thinking* about the emotion comes first.

THE PSYCHOLOGY
OF HOPE

We tend to feel hope when times are tough but we can envisage the possibility of a better future. Like interest, hope is often a motivator. Psychologist Barbara Fredrickson explains that hope helps us focus on our ability to overcome obstacles and sets into action our resourcefulness.[26] Hope builds optimism and resilience in the face of the hardships we all sometimes experience.

The late psychologist Charles R. Snyder and his colleagues developed a theory about the fundamental building blocks of hope.[27] They explored how it works as a profound manner of human coping and, more than this, of thriving. Snyder's "Hope Theory" shows that, psychologically speaking, hope and hopeful thinking have three characteristics, which most of us can probably recognize.

IN SNYDER'S THEORY, HOPE IS DEFINED BY:

1	2	3
the goal	*the pathway*	*agency*
WANTING SOMETHING	CREATING A ROUTE TO THAT GOAL	ACTING TOWARD THE GOAL

Hopeful thinking here is the combination of *envisioning our goals*, along with the ability or determination to *create and follow that pathway*. If little Katie wants a new tree house, this is her goal; but to be truly hopeful that this goal will become a reality, Katie has to both imagine *how* she might get the tree house (probably by pleading with her parents) and *believe in herself* enough to take steps in this direction (approaching her parents with a strong case.)

If Katie meets obstacles along this path (if she finds, for example, that Mum and Dad simply do not have enough time after work to be labouring in the back garden), then, to continue living in hope and not be defeated, she must imagine further pathways toward the goal (perhaps she can ask Grandad instead – he has lots of free time) and act determinedly (asking her parents if she can bring her plea to Grandad.)

You may notice that Hope Theory involves a lot of thinking. You would be right. The theory does emphasize a *cognitive* rather than an *emotional* process. This is not to say we do not feel hope as an emotion, but that we feel the emotion as a result of our hopeful thinking. Does this chime with your own experience? Take a few minutes now to think about your own definition of hope.

Whether or not you agree that our emotions come out of our cognitive, thinking processes – and there is some argument about this among psychologists – there is definitely plenty of interesting fodder here for writing hope in our journals. We can use a journal to map out this thinking process for ourselves, and the feelings that surround it. A journal is a place to dwell on hope in terms of both our thoughts *and* our feelings.

A STORY OF
WRITING HOPE

To frame John's experience of positive journalling, let me share the story of how the two of us met, because it offers an interesting context. I was lucky enough to meet John when he brought himself along to a series of weekly meetings I had organized, on the topic of positive psychology, when I was living in Barcelona. I wanted to meet some like-minded people and so set up this group as a way to talk about different aspects of the psychology of happiness, every Sunday afternoon over a cup of tea. John was, in fact, the very first member of this unusual little club and the first to illustrate a surprising fact that became obvious in the following weeks and months: that it was often the quiet, studious group members like him, not the more openly enthusiastic and opinionated, who would come time and again to the discussion group.

What might we interpret from this? Perhaps just that the space offered an easy way for these less naturally sociable characters to socialize. Yet it also shows that positive emotions do not always bubble to the surface in a way that is easy to perceive. Someone can be enjoying an activity – just as John and the other quieter members enjoyed the discussion group – but this does not necessarily manifest itself in grins, guffaws or bold gesticulations. Instead, it can take the form of a quiet commitment: turning up to the group, time and again, to participate coolly in the discussion.

This sheds a light on positive journalling. Positivity is not all gleaming smiles and upbeat affirmations – and if you think of it purely this way you have probably found yourself shirking away from the whole idea at times, unable to relate. Positivity comes in many other guises. When we recognize this, we see that beliefs such as "I am not a naturally positive person" may be misguided: we may simply have set limited parameters for what we call positive.

What is more, this example of the quiet-yet-more-committed members of the group provides an interesting context to the way John went about his writing as part of The Positive Journalling Study.

CASE STUDY

John

_____

When John talked about how writing for the study had gone for him, he was a bit concerned about having done it "wrong", because, as he explained, it had been about "more thoughts than feelings", more of a "brain" activity than an emotional one. He also spoke about how his positive journalling gave him a new perspective – how interesting it was that this way of writing had made him look at a particular experience in a new light. "I looked at... the event," he said, "in a different way than I probably would have done some years ago." There was no "wrong" way that John could have written, and his approach – being slightly different from that of the other participants – was actually a very intriguing one. When asked to talk about this in more detail, he mentioned that he had not been describing his feelings in the writing (this was what he imagined to be the "right" way to go about it), but instead he was "using the feeling to think about something".

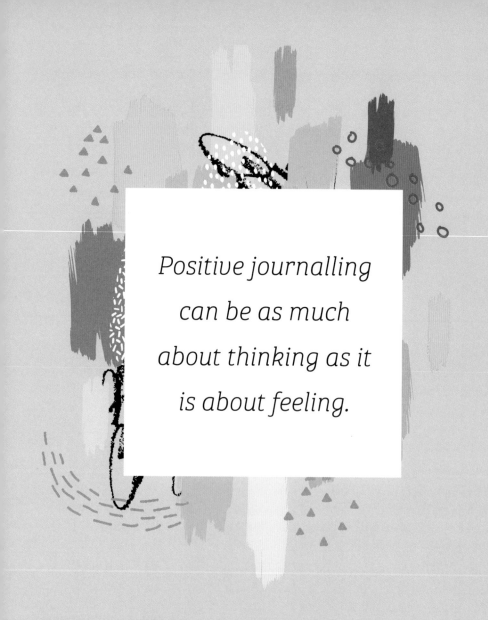

Positive journalling can be as much about thinking as it is about feeling.

Journalling is such a personal activity that it would be foolish to think that one way of doing it would suit everyone. Interestingly, John's experience of positive journalling backs up those psychologists who talk about hope as a thinking process, and shows that positive journalling can be as much about thinking as it is about feeling.

As far as I know, John was not aware of Hope Theory, which makes his emphasis on the thought process of using hope in his journal writing all the more interesting. Importantly, by doing this, John was not doing the exercise "wrong". Just because he did not feel moved to jump for joy and reach an ecstatic level of glee in the writing, that doesn't mean he failed to achieve this ephemeral, hallowed thing we call positivity. His cool, analytical style was just as positive as that of any other person in the study. This is worth remembering if you, too, find you tend to be more thought-focused than feeling-focused in your journal writing. We will never do positivity – or positive journalling – wrong, just differently.

John's story emphasizes another important facet of positive journalling: the change in perspective it offers us. A great many of the people in the study said that what had happened to John had happened to them, too. Because we don't tend to write in the "key" of positivity, when we do it is perhaps not surprising that we experience our writing – and what we are writing about – differently. This means that a relatively simple change can make an enormous shift: writing with positive emotions can help us to see our lives a whole new way.

When we recount our day, our week or a more distant period of our life in terms of our positive emotions, we are offered the chance to reframe things – perhaps in a way that is far more illuminating, helpful or constructive than our default interpretation. Journalling with positive emotions, as much as anything else, gives us the option to "try on" these different perspectives for size.

TAKEAWAY LESSONS

1

WE DO NOT ALWAYS HAVE TO START BY TRYING TO *FEEL* POSITIVE EMOTIONS IN OUR WRITING; WE CAN SIMPLY *THINK ABOUT* THEM.

In fact, positive feelings may well be a happy consequence of writing somewhat more thoughtfully and analytically. If you find that you cannot access any of the emotions in this book immediately when writing about them, try pondering them in a slightly more intellectual way: what do they mean? What do you think about the emotion? Perhaps even think about the etymology of the emotion. This may provide a way in to feeling it.

2

THERE IS NO WAY TO DO POSITIVITY WRONG.

We should allow ourselves to be surprised by positivity and the different shades it comes in. Positive journalling can be the perfect way to emphasize this. The quiet and analytical person can be just as positive as the loud and jubilant one – and may even display a deeper level of commitment. The understated emotion of hope is just as profoundly positive as vivacious joy – we just have to change the way we think about it. And, with that in mind...

3 WRITING WITH POSITIVE EMOTIONS IS A WAY TO CHALLENGE OUR PERSPECTIVES, EVEN THOSE LONG-HELD ONES.

Simply placing a different frame around an experience can significantly alter the way you feel about it. The positive emotions in this book offer a selection of different frames to try. This is not about forcing a difficult time into the box in our brains titled "Happy Memories". It is simply about exploration; it is about not being fixed to any single interpretation of the events of our lives, but rather being flexible and open-minded to the nuances of human emotional life.

TEN WAYS TO WRITE WITH **HOPE**

It is time to delve into another bundle of writing exercises that you can try. In earlier chapters we talked about the importance of detail and description in positive journalling as a way to evoke the emotion you are writing with. If that has been working well for you, then by all means continue in this vein. But if you have felt something forced about this, or perhaps sensed some vital step missing, here is an opportunity to take John's approach and be a bit more thought-focused.

This could mean asking things like "What causes me to feel this?" Or "For what purpose?" Or "Where do I want to go next with this?" You might even like to think of whatever you write about in terms of Hope Theory: how do your goals, goal pathways and motivation play a part in how you experience hope?

Let's jump in.

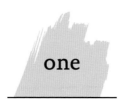

one

WRITE ABOUT A TIME IN THE PAST WHEN YOU FELT HOPEFUL. Perhaps something went dreadfully wrong, yet you saw the proverbial light at the end of the tunnel and kept going. It might have been the end of a significant relationship, a health problem or any other event that left you feeling powerless or overwhelmed, but where you were able to imagine a better future on the horizon – a horizon you may well now be living. Write about this in detail.

two

WRITE ABOUT A FUTURE, OR AN ASPECT OF YOUR FUTURE, THAT YOU ARE HOPEFUL ABOUT. Are you confident about passing with flying colours, reaching a milestone or surmounting an obstacle? What pathway are you following to get there? Write about why you think you are so motivated by hope in this particular area of your life, and perhaps how this hopefulness could infiltrate other areas, where you might feel less self-assured.

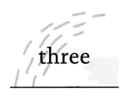

three

FIND HOPE IN THE PRESENT MOMENT. Hope, by its very nature, is a future-focused emotion – so "finding hope in the present" is something of a paradox. But we can regard hopeful thinking as beginning with little seedlings, so small that they might at first be imperceptible. By mindfully looking for hope in the now, we may discover seedlings we did not know were there. See if you can mine for a glimmer of hope in your current circumstances. If you have seen a great failure, where might hope be beginning to take root, even now? Perhaps it is simply a renewed sense of humility. If the situation looks dire, can you sense hope being stirred by the support of good friends? Remember to take care with this, and be compassionate rather than pushy with yourself.

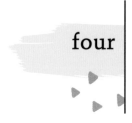

four

WRITE ABOUT A PERSON WHO MAKES YOU PARTICULARLY HOPEFUL. This might be a close relative or friend, or perhaps a favourite journalist or musician whose slant always gives you a sense of better things to come. Write in detail about how this person evokes hope for you. A powerful quotation or poem might serve you well as a prompt here, such as Emily Dickinson's poem "Hope is the thing with feathers".

five

WRITE ABOUT WHAT HOPE FEELS LIKE, LOOKS LIKE, TASTES LIKE OR SMELLS LIKE. Is hope a seductive shade of silver or a bright and sunny yellow? Does it taste syrupy or zesty? Could you even think of hope as a creature, such as Emily Dickinson's "thing with feathers" or a spider continually spinning its web in the wind? Let any new metaphors sit with you for a while, then ask, "Which one feels poignant?" This may well form the basis of a more creative piece of writing, such as a poem, and that is great if so. There are no rules to this thing called writing.

six

WRITE ABOUT HOW YOU COULD THINK OF HOPE DIFFERENTLY. Hope Theory is just one very specific, scientific model on a topic that has kept philosophers and other great thinkers intrigued for eons. There is always room for a different version, interpretation or construction of hope. You might want to begin by focusing on how hope can be found in unexpected places, and go from there.

seven

WRITE ABOUT HOW OTHERS MIGHT FIND HOPE IN YOU. Writing can be a very introspective act, but we rarely use it specifically to focus on our good qualities – the things that make us, and other human beings, great. By focusing on these qualities, we give ourselves a better chance to cultivate them. Offering hope to one another is a thing that we humans do very well. Do you believe you offer anyone hope? Perhaps you made a donation to a charity or offered a kind word to someone who was struggling. Write about further ways you could offer hope to others.

eight

WRITE ABOUT HOW YOU COULD BEGIN A DAILY PRACTICE OF HOPE. We all know those dreary days where things seem only bleaker than they are pitiful. Yet a small daily act of hope can be a preventative gesture against these universally experienced moments of woe. It might be reading a few pages – even just one page – of a book that gives you a sense of hope. I like the humanistic psychologists for this, such as Abraham Maslow's *Toward a Psychology of Being*. For something more creative, try Walt Whitman's astonishing *Leaves of Grass*. Or take a different approach and make the effort to centre at least one of your conversations a day on hope for the future. What other hopeful practices can you think of?

nine

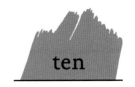

ten

WRITE ABOUT FINDING HOPE IN YOUR SURROUNDINGS. Write about how the natural or urban world offers you a sense of hope. For example, although I know not everyone feels this way, I feel hopeful when I see wind farms on the horizon: "We might one day be 100 per cent sustainable after all," I ponder, and, if we aren't, at least there were people in the world who tried. Perhaps ancient mountains give you a sense of perspective, and you can feel hopeful about your part in a bigger story. Try and think of your own examples, and explain how and why they give you hope.

WRITE ABOUT HOPE IN RELATION TO YOUR GOALS. We talked earlier about how goals are integral to Hope Theory. Why not try writing more generally about your own current goals in terms of hope? In what ways are they tied up with hope? How has hope played a part in your past goals? Maybe you think hope can exist free of any fixed goals. If so, explore this in your writing.

Writing
Pride

Writing is always a statement. It is a statement about what we have seen and who we are, a statement about where we have been and where we might want to go. Writing can be a statement of faith – in our dreams, in others, in ourselves – or even a statement that we are ready to give up. Often, we write to state what we need or want – perhaps even what we are desperate for. Yet what about writing to state what we already have? Or to cultivate a sense of fulfilment about the life we are living? What if our writing was a statement of our pride?

Pride has classically been thought of as a sin – the opposite of humility – but the two are actually quite separate emotional experiences, each with a golden mean of its own. Pride is sometimes associated with self-centredness or even outright vanity, but an overactive sense of self-effacement or shame about who we are can be equally self-centred: in either case, the concentration is on ourselves.

Feeling pride is actually a very common and appropriate human response to life. We feel it in many everyday scenarios: when we win at cards or complete a painting we like or cook a wonderful meal. In many cultures, we have been conditioned to repress our pride because too much of it can make others uncomfortable. However, if a friend was really proud of a soufflé he had whipped up, few of us would object. Just the right amount of pride – which of course varies with context and person – can be a valuable tool in the emotional arsenal, because it is yet another of our motivating feelings. What would drive us, as a species, to complete exquisite architectural triumphs, or to perfect epic musical scores, or even to be altruistic, were it not for the desire to take a little pride in who we are and what we have achieved?

There is a term for excessive pride: hubris. It is what brings down Shakespearean heroes and has caused the fall of many of our greatest empires. Yet, just as we do not shun love because obsession exists, why would we shun pride because hubris exists? More than this, when people describe pride as "sinful", it doesn't account for the great pride we can feel for others – whether it is our children succeeding in something at school, or a sports figure doing well in representing our country. This is a valid dimension of the emotion of pride, and an important way that we bond with others, within our close families and wider communities.

THE PSYCHOLOGY OF PRIDE

Psychologists have called pride one of our "self-conscious emotions" – along with guilt, shame and embarrassment.[28] Given this list, we can see how self-conscious emotions are not often very positive! Yet two leading researchers in the psychology of pride, Jessica Tracy at the University of British Columbia and Richard Robins at the University of California, Davis, have identified two forms of pride: what they call *hubristic* and *authentic.*[29]

What this means is that, as long as our pride is authentic (that is, it makes us friendly go-getters and not self-centred bozos), there is no need to feel shame over it. One great feature of authentic pride is that it urges us on to more ambitious goals.[30] If we succeed at a soufflé, for example, we might plan a three-course dinner for friends. Appropriateness to our pride is particularly important here. There will usually be some social value to what our culture says we can acceptably feel pride for – which, thankfully, is what stops most of us from becoming arrogant megalomaniacs who take pride in destroying children's sandcastles or keeping seats from elderly people on the bus.

Pride helps us both to establish ourselves socially, as valued members of a given group, and to drive us to strive toward bigger and better achievements. Both of these are integral to thriving in our lives. What are your own thoughts about the difference between authentic and hubristic pride? Take the time now to think about how you define this emotion.

Based on the psychology behind pride, if we can self-generate a greater sense of authentic pride through our writing, it seems like a good idea that we should.

As long as our pride is authentic, there is no need to feel shame over it.

A STORY OF WRITING PRIDE

Rita had been on a journey of what she called "personal change work" with a psychotherapist for several years, and had previously used a journal to support her wellbeing.

CASE STUDY

Rita

Rita was reading about the first gay weddings in England when she chose to write with pride. "I was thinking about all the pride that was on display in the news videos," she said. "I was thinking how pride would play a part in my life... what I'm proud of accomplishing in my life, and noting down when others have said they are proud of me." Rita described what she saw as a certain amount of nuance to pride – that it is not a purely positive emotion – and so it brought up some mixed emotions for her. She found that many emotions – including pride – "could be positive or negative or mixed" and that "there are lots of shades of grey, or colours of the rainbow..." She also described being creative in her journal: "I could feel myself wanting to write a poem on all three occasions," she said. "My prose started turning into something more poetic... I think if I had continued I would have written poems."

> *Writing with pride may help to give a greater sense of how we fit – positively – in a community context.*

Rita shows that we do tend to think about pride in a somewhat self-conscious way, as psychologists suggest. She does not, however, appear to be hubristic in her sense of pride. In fact, her first instinct was to link pride with others, given the occasion of the first gay weddings in England. Even when she does begin to say how she focused on herself, and that she thought of accomplishments she herself was proud of, she also explores instances when others have said they are proud of her. Again, Rita's story confirms what psychologists tell us: that pride reinforces our "pro-social" behaviour – helpful behaviour intended to foster friendships with others – and is intertwined with our social status. Rita thinks of herself, but she very much thinks of herself *in context* – and this is an important distinction. We are social creatures and many – if not most – of our positive emotions highlight this. If you needed more evidence that a positive personal journalling practice is not "selfish" even if it is "self-conscious", then here you have it. We tend to be self-conscious of ourselves primarily in a community context, and writing with pride may help to give a greater sense of how we fit positively in this context.

Rita also talked about the nuance of the positive emotions upon which the study had asked her to reflect. She mentioned specifically that her writing about pride "was mixed, there was a lot of anger". Some of us can feel uncomfortable at the suggestion to "be positive" because it seems to negate other emotional experiences. This need not be the case at all. Rita described that she went very deeply into her "current feelings on certain things" and was "very happy" that she could put those feelings into a journal. It can be helpful, especially in our journal practice, to think of our emotional experiences as cocktails. The appropriate anger that Rita felt, mixed with her pride, may be a very motivating combination given her circumstances. No emotion, even our most positive, is one-dimensional, because the experience of being a human is not one-dimensional. We are vastly complex, and so our emotions often manifest in complex ways. This complexity, in all its shades, has a place in our journal.

Another intriguing approach that Rita took in her positive journalling was to veer toward a more creative style of writing. In the same way, you may begin to feel your writing becoming more artistic. Perhaps you will want to bring in rhyme, explore some imagery or even create characters. If you are not someone who typically writes creatively, this might feel odd or self-indulgent. Yet playing creatively with, and even fictionalizing from, our experience in positive journalling has many benefits. Not only is creative writing a lot of fun, but it also asks us to explore our experience in new ways – to redraft, to alchemize and perhaps to form new beliefs about that experience. All of this can have a knock-on effect for our happiness.

TAKEAWAY LESSONS

1 **JOURNALLING WITH POSITIVE EMOTIONS, PARTICULARLY PRIDE, MIGHT BE SELF-CONSCIOUS, BUT THIS IS OFTEN IN THE CONTEXT OF OTHERS.**

Think about it: how would we experience consciousness of the "self" without consciousness of "others"? We simply could not. Just as we would not know what "hot" was without "cold". The emotion of pride can lead us to think about how others show their pride, as well as occasions when those close to us have shown pride in us – perhaps as a "thermometer" for feeling pride about ourselves in a way that is more objectively accurate. We do not *have* to write about others when we write about our pride, but it appears we may do this quite naturally.

2

POSITIVE EMOTIONS CAN BE EXPERIENCED AS "COCKTAILS".

Most of our emotional experiences are nuanced and diverse, and that is great! Though we might want to begin with a positive emotion prompt in journal writing, this does not by any means exclude an exploration of our more negative emotions. Pride may lead to anger, which may lead back to pride or even to another positive emotion such as hope. Emotions tend to come in blends, like a delicately infused herbal tea. Most of us can relate, for example, to feeling both deeply happy about something and, at the same time, subtly sad about the experience ending. The aim of positive journalling is not to supress our valid negative emotions, which can themselves be incredibly motivating, but simply to round out the writing experience to something beyond a cathartic letting go of difficult feelings, to something that also builds up resources. Viewing our emotional experiences as multidimensional is one way to begin this.

3

POSITIVE JOURNALLING CAN NATURALLY LEAD TO MORE CREATIVE FORMS OF WRITING.

Whether you typically write creatively or not, you may find that exploring your emotions through words on a page stirs your poetic sensibilities. Run with this if and when it happens – so long as the conventions of creative writing do not begin to feel limiting. Writing poetically can be a lovely way to capture the detail and metaphorical nature of our emotions, and there are other forms of creative writing that may arise out of journalling, such as memoir. As long as this does not limit you (writing creatively can often do the opposite, and actually enhance a writing experience), then do not feel that your journal space is not the "correct" place for creativity.

TEN WAYS TO WRITE WITH PRIDE

How might you use pride in your own writing practice? Again, rich detail and description in your positive journalling are good starting points. You might want to write about the nuances of how pride feels: does it reside somewhere specific in the body? Does the sensation stir and gently increase, or does it burst upon you all at once? Is it usually lasting, or brief? Try to capture all of this detail, and more, in your writing.

one

WRITE ABOUT A TIME IN THE PAST FOR WHICH YOU FELT, OR STILL FEEL, PRIDE. Is there an achievement, great or small, that you would like to recall in your writing? What was the source of the pride: that you persevered? That you helped others? That you outdid yourself? Dwell on why and how you felt this experience of pride, and what you might learn from this now.

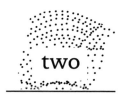

two

WRITE ABOUT A FUTURE TIME WHEN YOU ANTICIPATE YOU WILL FEEL PRIDE. Are you working toward a specific goal or achievement, such as a course of study, in which you expect to do well? Explore what anticipating pride feels like, while taking care not to become too attached to the outcome. We cannot usually control how things turn out, though we can put in our best effort – and that is always something to be proud of.

three

FIND PRIDE IN THE PRESENT MOMENT. Are you feeling stronger because of regular exercise, or are you proud of your ability to cope with something difficult that is going on, despite how hard it has been? Explore your sense of pride for that. Pride can be very motivating as we look to the future, but it is also good practice to draw your sense of pride back to the present moment and to think of what makes you proud of yourself *right now*. You can be proud to be vulnerable, proud to be strong, proud to be here after everything, proud of being a good friend, mother, brother or partner... Shine the torch of pride on whatever or whoever it is that you are right now.

four

WRITE ABOUT SOMEONE YOU FEEL PRIDE IN.
Others can make us feel a great deal of pride.
It might be someone you know intimately, such
as a spouse achieving his or her goals, or a child
doing well in school. Equally, though, it might be
someone you have never met, such as a sports
hero, a political activist or an environmental
researcher on a mission to save the planet. It
might be anyone from a socially motivated artist
you admire to your grandmother who is battling
through bereavement. It might be the service
people in your city – the health workers keeping
people well and the rubbish collectors keeping
the streets clean. Human activity is a great
web of interdependence, which is something we
sometimes forget. Pride can help us to remember.
Why do you feel pride in this person or group,
and how? Does your pride in them make you feel
more proud of humans generally, and what we
can achieve together? Write about what you might
learn from this feeling of pride.

five

WRITE ABOUT WHAT PRIDE FEELS LIKE, LOOKS LIKE, TASTES LIKE OR SMELLS LIKE. You can think of pride as shiny or matte, glowing gold or a pure gentle white. Pride might feel heavy, or like a comforting hug. It might have the scent of polished trophies from the past, or the aroma of early morning coffee as you rise to face another day. Thinking of pride in these unusual ways can help you to connect to the emotion in a novel way, and so potentially in a reinvigorated and even deeper way. Explore pride with all your senses in your writing, and then perhaps write about why you think you experience pride in this way.

six

WRITE ABOUT HOW YOU COULD THINK OF PRIDE DIFFERENTLY. Pride does not have to swell in your chest. You can be proud of achievements both great and small. Pride is a single person giving a thumbs-up as much as it is a standing ovation. And pride is not only a pat on the back from another, but can sometimes just be a discreet belief in yourself. Write about how you currently define pride, and how you might extend this definition.

seven

WRITE ABOUT HOW OTHERS MIGHT FEEL PROUD OF YOU. This exercise might make you feel uncomfortable if you tend to be self-effacing, but it is an interesting way of shifting your view of yourself to one that is more objective. Even if you struggle to get a sense of how others might be proud of you, do not be deterred. Most of us are striving to be the kind of person others are proud of – but this can be a long journey and it is okay not to be there yet. If you feel more confident, you might want to augment this exercise by asking someone close to you what *they* are proud of in you.

WRITE ABOUT HOW YOU COULD BEGIN A DAILY PRACTICE OF PRIDE. If this seems self-indulgent, then think about shifting your sense of pride out to others. Yet I do encourage you also to include a practice of taking pride in yourself. Remember: this is *authentic* and not *hubristic* pride. Ground it in reality. Be proud you got through a difficult day, proud of the nutritious meal you made even if you did not feel like cooking, proud of being a good friend to someone who needed you. A practice can be as simple as a few words of affirmation to yourself, a few lines written in your journal or making the effort to tell others you are proud of them. Write in detail about how daily pride might feel and how it might change the day, if at all.

eight

nine

WRITE ABOUT FEELING PRIDE IN YOUR SURROUNDINGS. It may sound trite, but generating a sense of pride in Mother Nature may actually be extremely valuable as a way of transcending the self and of appreciating the larger biological system within which we exist. Of course, Nature does not care how we feel about her, but feeling proud of our miraculous ecosystem – of the atmosphere keeping us cool or the hardworking trees creating our oxygen – might help us to take note of our interdependency with all other things, and to behave accordingly: in proud recognition of the planet we call home.

ten

WRITE ABOUT PRIDE AND SOCIAL CONNECTION. As well as feeling proud of others, the feeling that we are worthy of taking pride in ourselves has an important social function, because it gives us a better sense of our social standing. Write about how someone who is proud of their achievements might fit in a social group – remembering not to confuse pride with vanity. Pride can be quiet and subtle, and may just translate as a person being happy with who they are. How does pride work in one-to-one friendships? Or among larger groups, such as colleagues in an office? Or even on a national, cultural or global scale? Write your thoughts about one or all of these, thinking about pride's links with social connection.

Writing
Awe

Writing is a form of curiosity. A hand with a pen in it has a life of its own, and sometimes it is simply our job to sit back and see what happens. We can surprise ourselves with the words we write, because they are often not quite what we anticipated. Writing is endlessly intriguing for this reason, and is a great practice for generating feelings of awe and wonder at the world and our place in it.

Awe is one of our most beautiful and thrilling emotions. It is defined by reverence and overwhelm – which means it can often be missing in the ins and outs of the everyday. Have you felt it lately?

That expression to be "in awe" is noteworthy. Why do we say that we *feel* most emotions – but when it comes to love and awe, we are *in* them? Perhaps because these emotions are like marinades for the soul. They often hit us out of nowhere,

and suddenly we find ourselves dunked up to the neck in a physical–emotional experience. In this sense, awe is something of a spiritual emotion, but that does not mean one must be religious to experience it.

Awe is an emotion aroused by exceptional moments. One reason that many of us enjoy travel so much is that it stirs up our feelings of awe. We do not tend to feel in awe during the average week of work and trips to the supermarket and hanging out the washing – but awe is important for recalibrating our sense of reverence and for acknowledging our diminutive role in the theatre of the universe. This might seem odd to a Western, secular mind – humans are remarkable, so why should we feel diminutive? Well, for one, because we are the first mass culture with nothing to worship but ourselves – many of us have no gods to speak of, no system of beliefs in the mysterious. We have only the clinical rigour of our own science to comfort us. Not only is this dangerous – because it breeds *hubris*, which we looked at in the previous chapter on pride – but it is a lot of responsibility. In an individualistic culture we can often fall into the trap of berating ourselves for not achieving more, because we are supposedly all-powerful. We glance around and find no one to blame but ourselves. This can lead to a great deal of existential suffering. Awe is an antidote to this.

THE PSYCHOLOGY
OF AWE

Our feelings of awe are usually kindled when we encounter virtue, great beauty, huge size or immense power – whether this comes in the form of a person, place, tangible thing or even a concept.[31] These encounters often stir us to try to accommodate this impossible grandeur into our own self and world-view. Positive psychologists Dacher Keltner and Jonathan Haidt have written a lot about the emotion of awe.[32] "Awe is felt," they tell us, "about diverse events and objects, from waterfalls to childbirth to scenes of devastation" and "is central to the experience of religion, politics, nature, and art." Even though these experiences might be "fleeting and rare", they can often "change the course of a life in profound and permanent ways".

For these scientists, there are many events and objects that can "trigger" our sense of awe, including "religious encounters, charismatic political leaders, natural objects, and even patterns of darkness and light". Beautiful sunrises, the moonlit ocean and the aurora borealis all serve to stir feelings of awe in us. We even feel a range of what psychologists call "awe-related states", including "admiration, astonishment, and more mild feelings of beauty" that both "relate to and differ from each other".

There are two central components at the heart of feelings of awe; psychologists refer to them as *vastness* and *accommodation*. Vastness is something that is experienced as being far bigger than the individual self – though this is not limited to physical size, but can also mean social size, including celebrity and authority. Experiencing the majesty of Yosemite National Park matches this description, but so might witnessing the rally of a significant political figure. Take a couple of minutes here to pause and think about how you interpret the emotion of awe in your own life, or how you have experienced it.

Our world-view is often stretched by experience of awe. Awe stirs a need to try to integrate a new, previously unknown truth within ourselves. This need may or may not be fulfilled in an experience of awe. This is why feelings of great mystery often accompany this emotion – for example, in gazing at the stars and contemplating the wonders of the universe. We cannot quite relate to such vastness and can therefore never fully accommodate the stars within our world-view: they are, both literally and figuratively, out of our reach.

One thing is for certain about awe: it is a supremely powerful emotion. "Awe can transform people and reorient their lives, goals and values," say Dacher and Haidt, stressing that "awe-inducing events may be one of the fastest and most powerful methods of personal change and growth". This is exciting because it offers a stirring case for incorporating more awe into our lives, especially if this is not something we currently get to feel often.

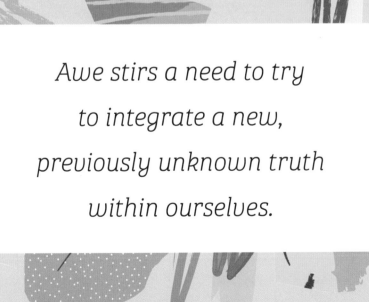

Awe stirs a need to try to integrate a new, previously unknown truth within ourselves.

A STORY OF WRITING AWE

When Mark kindly took part in the study, he was in his early twenties,
a continental European living in London and studying for a master's degree.
He was also one of several people in the study who chose to write with awe.

CASE STUDY

Mark

Mark explained that he was "drawn" to the emotion of awe. This, he said, was because it was not an emotion he would usually reflect on, but was nevertheless one that he felt was important. "I do not consciously think about what gives me awe," he added. "I hardly ever recognize if I am in awe... I couldn't actually tell you when was the last time that I felt in awe of something. Although I know I do sometimes." Mark felt this way about some of the other positive emotions he chose to write with, too. He described many of these emotions as aspects of his life that he was "not really aware of" or that he never thought much about. After writing with awe, Mark summed up the experience well by saying that "it put it on my radar... It gave me this perspective on a few things that are part of my life but have not really been part of my life at the same time – because I didn't notice them."

Mark's experience is probably something that a lot of us can empathize with. The fleeting nature of these emotions means they can pass by unnoticed or overlooked. Our negative emotions are bullies – we cannot ignore them because they march right up and hit us on the nose. Our more positive emotions tend to tiptoe up to us, imparting a subtle, warm glow that we take for granted. For this reason, we often fail to savour our positive emotions, which sometimes means that our negative feelings have a more noticeable effect on us. Mark's story offers us a really helpful way to look at positive journalling: it puts positive emotions on our radar.

When asked to compare positive journalling with his typical journal writing, Mark admitted, "It is not my main motivation to write a journal to feel positive emotions." This is probably true for most of us who have used journalling in our lives. As we have seen throughout this book, journalling has many different purposes, one of the most common being to "vent" or "dump" our negative emotions onto the page. Yet Mark's story showed that, when he did embrace the positive emotions, he "was able to write about things – in a way that I wouldn't usually". Because he did not normally look at his life in terms of his positive emotions, this way of writing offered a new perspective on aspects of his life. We can be motivated to journal for all manner of reasons; positive journalling is simply another tool in our arsenal. When he did use journalling to focus on his positive emotions, Mark echoed what many others in the study stressed, which was that, at times, he felt he self-generated the emotion in the writing: "I think I definitely experienced this emotion... through writing it, at least in some sentences – maybe not in all of them."

Mark also echoes what psychology tells us about awe: he appeared to adopt an altered world-view on certain topics. He explained that writing awe, and positive journalling more generally, felt like a tool to use on certain days, when he wanted to explore a new aspect of his life. Positive journalling offers a great way to explore the new. Of course, we do not *need* to explore new aspects of our life and world. Many of us could live quite comfortably for years never changing our world-view one iota. Yet, in a rapidly changing global culture, not only is changing our perspective now and again useful, it might be essential to enabling us to thrive as human beings.

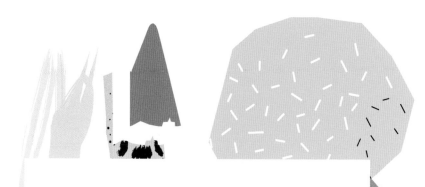

*We can be motivated
to journal for all
manner of reasons;
positive journalling
is simply another tool
in our arsenal.*

TAKEAWAY LESSONS

1

WRITING WITH POSITIVE EMOTIONS CAN PUT THESE EMOTIONS ON OUR RADAR.

Though most of us will probably experience a range of positive emotions on the average day, we often fail to take due note of all of them. Writing is an excellent method of taking note – and therefore of prioritizing these emotions. This can be really satisfying, and relatively easy as far as self-help techniques go, because we are not being asked to create emotional experiences from scratch: rather we are invited to mine our present lives for the dormant treasures already there. This is not about building, or planning, or motivating new habits into action – an aspect of much self-help that can leave us feeling overwhelmed and exhausted. It is simply about stopping to notice.

2

POSITIVE EMOTION DOES NOT HAVE TO BE OUR MAIN MOTIVATION TO JOURNAL, BUT IT CAN HELP.

Journals and journal writing should be flexible, inclusive and highly personal ways of engaging with our lives – tools for surmounting life's obstacles, as well as for helping us to thrive. A positive emotion such as awe is just one of many avenues to take in writing for this purpose. Do not think that you have to make positive journalling your main motivation for writing from here on – you do not. The main purpose of using positive emotions in your journal writing should simply be to balance out this practice; to make it more enjoyable, potentially more fulfilling and to help you prioritize your most treasured emotional experiences, such as awe.

3

WRITING WITH POSITIVE EMOTIONS HELPS US TO EXPLORE THE NEW.

Precisely because positive emotions are not the main motivation, or default option, for most of us to write in a journal, they can do the best job of taking us out of autopilot and helping us gain a fresh perspective on what might be going on in our lives. Most of us have had the experience of epiphany, to a greater or lesser extent. We often call these "light-bulb moments" – when things click together gloriously like a completed Rubik's Cube and we suddenly see a new way forward. Now, nobody is saying that positive journalling is a sure-fire way of facilitating epiphany – there is no such foolproof method of manufacturing these mini-miracles. Yet, by virtue of their novelty for most of us, using positive emotions in our writing can help us to think about our lives in an innovative, revealing way.

TEN WAYS TO WRITE WITH AWE

Writing awe is a beautiful concept, and it is something that poets do particularly well. Poets know the great beauty that can be found in the everyday minutiae of our lives – just take a look at Pablo Neruda's "Ode to a Lemon", for example – but we do not have to be poets to bring awe into our writing. Awe has the potential to become an active part of any journalling practice.

You will probably find that being detailed and descriptive is particularly useful for generating feelings of awe, because even the most ordinary-seeming things have glorious detail when we choose to look closely.

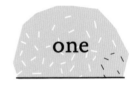

one

WRITE ABOUT A TIME IN THE PAST WHEN YOU FELT AWE. Experiences in nature are a good place to start if you are struggling to recall a moment of awe. Perhaps you can remember a magnificent sunset or a stunning landscape. How did it feel to witness this? You might have felt awe when holding your first-born or hearing the singing of a wonderful choir. Write about how this felt and what it meant to you.

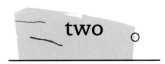
two

WRITE ABOUT A FUTURE TIME WHEN YOU ANTICIPATE YOU WILL FEEL AWE. This may seem a little odd because awe, perhaps more than any other positive emotion, tends to arise uncalculatedly. Even so, writing this way may help you to narrow down why and how you experience awe. As a good starting point, think about a future occasion that will be "larger than yourself"– a concert you are looking forward to attending, perhaps. Or write about how you could think like a poet in your everyday life, and notice the miraculous details of your daily world. Perhaps tomorrow you might pay particular attention to the changing clouds and find awe in their grandeur.

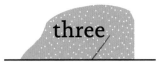

three

WRITE ABOUT YOUR AWE FOR THE PRESENT MOMENT. If you are sitting in your office cafeteria on a rainy Tuesday under fluorescent lights, this may be tricky. Yet the goal here is not to magically manufacture awe, but to explore its inner workings and nuances. Speaking of inner workings: why not write in awe of your body and the work going on in your cells and organs right now to keep you alive, with no input from your active will. Or, if you really are in the cafeteria at work, write about your awe for the organized systems humans have built in order to work together and create together.

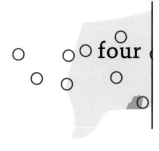

four

WRITE ABOUT A PERSON YOU ARE IN AWE OF. This is a wonderful way to view other humans. We can be in awe of other people's courage or their kindness or their resilience. Even the most "ordinary" of individuals can be an endless expedition of awe if you think of the tiny form they had when arriving in this world as a baby, and how much they have grown, both literally and figuratively, just by virtue of being alive. All of us have had to show resilience, from overcoming traumas to our subtle survival of the everyday. Let your mind marvel at the vastness of another individual, and write about how this feels.

five

WRITE ABOUT WHAT AWE FEELS LIKE, LOOKS LIKE, TASTES LIKE OR SMELLS LIKE. How might you describe this in more metaphorical terms? Is awe a slow sunrise, spreading watercolour shades of pink and orange across a grey sky until the heavy orb of the sun ignites into bright day? Does it sound like an exultant church choir or the simultaneous beat of a hundred tribal drums? Is awe a ripe, scented citrus fruit or the disarming salt smell of a vast ocean? Write to forge some metaphors of your own.

six

WRITE ABOUT HOW YOU COULD THINK OF AWE DIFFERENTLY. Awe seems like a huge, almost otherworldly, kind of emotion. Yet, just as with the other emotions in this book, this need not be so – we just have to decide to look at it differently. Contemporary science has shown us the little atomic and sub-atomic universe that exists within even a tiny grain of sand – and that the vastness we experience on Earth is a veritable grain of sand in the context of the huge expanse of the universe. The point being that grandeur is relative. Does that help you to think of awe differently? Write about the awe-inspiring nature of the minuscule.

seven

WRITE ABOUT HOW OTHERS MAY BE IN AWE OF YOU.
This might seem self-indulgent for the more humble
among us, but give it a try. The key is to honour a
positive, objective view of ourselves that we may
not always see – without getting lost in hubris, as
we talked about in the previous chapter on pride.
What are you capable of, however small it seems,
that others struggle with? Are you an incredible
parent, unerringly loyal friend or courageous world-
traveller? Our own skills become commonplace to us,
but they can inspire awe in others for whom these
same skills do not come so naturally. Begin writing
about yourself from this perspective – you may even
like to try writing in the third person.

eight

WRITE ABOUT HOW YOU COULD BEGIN A DAILY
PRACTICE OF AWE. Again, awe has a flavour of
spontaneity somewhat stronger than other positive
emotions. Even so, attempting to facilitate mini-
experiences of awe in your daily life may still be
a worthwhile task. Spending time admiring nature,
or reflecting or meditating on your awe for others,
or exploring particularly awe-inspiring photography
like that in *National Geographic* magazine would
all be good practices. Can you think of other ways
to experience awe daily? Write them, write why and
write how daily awe might have an effect on your life.

nine

WRITE ABOUT FEELING AWE FOR YOUR SURROUNDINGS. I have mentioned the wild natural world as a source of awe several times in this chapter, because of its incredible vastness and beauty. Yet architecture can also inspire awe. Have you ever stood at the foot of the Duomo in Florence or the Sagrada Familia in Barcelona, for example? Even the rather unassuming Severn Bridge linking England and Wales once incited a feeling of awe in me when I took a moment to marvel at the engineering behind such a feat. Find spaces close to home that arouse your awe. From bluebells carpeting a forest floor to mind-boggling accomplishments of engineering – it all counts.

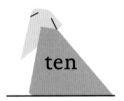

ten

WRITE ABOUT AWE AS INTEGRATION. In Keltner and Haidt's description of awe, both *vastness* and *accommodation* make up the experience. Accommodation – or integration – is a helpful word for thinking about how new ideas and experiences enter our lives. New ideas are like guests, both invited and uninvited, into the lodging house of our consciousness. Where shall we put them? Will they take pride of place in the presidential suite or get stuffed away into the broom cupboard? Awe functions, more often than not, to accommodate the miraculous within us. We feel it when we witness intense excellence or goodness. Write about how you integrate such experiences into your life: do they help you believe in a positive future for the human race, for example? Do they help you to feel more "at one" with others and your surroundings? Spend some time thinking and writing about how experiences of awe have altered your world-view.

Writing
Love

Writing is a craft and a vocation. It has long been a way that humans have busied themselves in the world. We use writing both to console and to criticize, to incite change and to cement old ways of doing things. Sometimes, though, we simply do it for the love of it.

If we were visitors from another planet sent to observe humans, I think we might be most struck by how often these curious Earth creatures busy themselves in activities purely for the love of it, as well as committing themselves to the occupation of giving love and being loved. One reason for this is that love offers us one of the most profound ways to feel a sense of belonging and meaning.

This chapter arrives last for a reason. That reason is one that you may find heart-warming: almost all of the people involved in The Positive Journalling Study chose love on at least one of the days of writing. More than this – it was the only emotion to be picked twice by any one person. In the emotion world, you could say love is kind of a big deal. Do we have any hope of describing such an all-embracing emotion on the page? Is love not something we *experience* rather than narrate? Well, yes and no is the answer to both of these questions.

Articulating what we feel can often *reinforce* what we feel. We find sense and shape for our experience through turning it into words. Sometimes, these are the words of another. We choose moving poems to read at emotional events such as weddings and funerals, because they articulate better than we can what the event causes us to feel. There is a particular power, however, in forming these words ourselves: not least because it gives us a sense of our own capability to understand and rewrite our experience, but also because we are usually the experts of our own experience.

For that reason, elaborating on our own ideas about love by committing them to the page is a worthwhile activity. We may never fully capture the immensity of an emotion like love, but we can liken it to taking a snapshot of clouds in the sky: we have not caught the whole universe, but we have crystallized a beautiful part of it that we can keep in our back pocket.

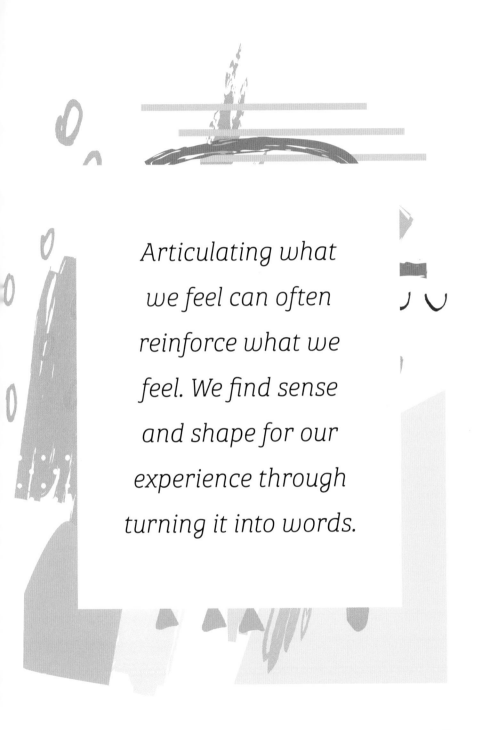

Articulating what we feel can often reinforce what we feel. We find sense and shape for our experience through turning it into words.

THE PSYCHOLOGY OF LOVE

It is important to keep in mind how even our most magnificent emotions are made up of tiny little daily experiences. Psychologist Barbara Fredrickson talks about our positive emotions in terms of *micro-moments*.[33] Although these moments are brief, they serve to powerfully affect and even define our lives. This is an important way to look at our positive emotions: as tiny little puzzle pieces, spilled across the days and weeks and years of our lives, that come together over time to fundamentally change who we are: influencing everything from whom we marry to our career choices. Positive journalling is one way to put these puzzle pieces together.

Writing with love, or with any other positive emotion, may help you to reflect on, savour and even *generate* that emotion for yourself – but the actual experience of the emotion will probably be fleeting. Once you shut your journal and get back to your day, the normal stressors we all experience will still be there (and the negative emotions that come with them!). Yet this does not mean your time has been wasted. Think of it this way: positive emotions work a bit like Vitamin C. The body does not store this vitamin as it does other vitamins. This is why we have to ensure a good supply daily. Equally, we could say that our minds do not "store" positive emotions. Therefore we would also do well to ensure a good daily supply of these micro-moments. In this way, we can embrace the fleeting nature of these wonderful emotions, not lament it.

Take a few moments here to reflect on how you experience love.

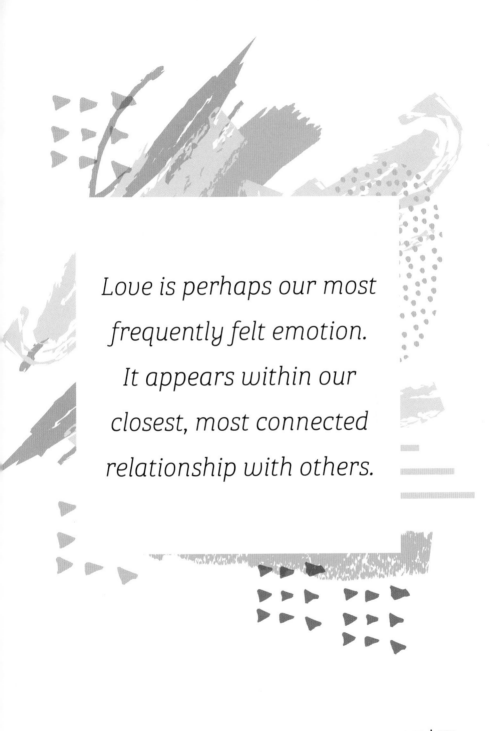

Love is perhaps our most frequently felt emotion. It appears within our closest, most connected relationship with others.

Love is perhaps our most frequently felt emotion. It appears within our closest, most connected relationships with others. We often experience love as a kind of self-expansion, strengthening our bonds with others and our sense of community.[34] In fact, when we use these emotions in our writing, one of the most exciting findings from The Positive Journalling Study was the "bridge" effect of these emotions.

With their typical journal writing, people used the page to vent their negative emotions. They described this as a very one-way trajectory of the "input" of life experience and the "output" of this onto the page. In other words: they felt *relieved* by the writing. In my study, they did something else. Using positive emotions offered them a kind of bridge, in two ways:

These journallers were better able to relate what they were writing to their daily lives – rather than only reacting to life, they were interacting with it, questioning it, prodding and poking it. They seemed to plan future actions based on what they were writing. In doing so, they created a bridge between the private inner world explored on the page, and the outer world, with a sense of their own ability to meet challenges.

The positive emotions appeared to promote a relation to others – they created a bridge of connection between these writers and those around them. Love (along with many of our other positive emotions) really does seem to be, as the Persian poet Rumi said many centuries ago, a bridge that unites us with everything else.

This bridge effect gives a sense of progress, and not just the feeling of having processed the tough stuff. It stirs up feelings of general positivity, but also of capability. John said that, through having done the writing, he felt more capable and as if he had "more good things to offer". Laura wrote a list of things she anticipated feeling proud of in the future. Rose said that she "came out of it feeling more positive", as if she had "made some progress". Even when Amanda "found it really difficult" to relate to the positive emotions and, in her own words, "resisted it quite a lot", she read back on her journal writing to discover that, retrospectively, she could see the benefit of it, because it made her notice the good things that *were* present in her life.

Thinking of good things in their lives did not mean that these writers only dwelled introspectively on themselves. The bridging effect from the page to real action was often expressed in relation to others. When the positive emotions, particularly love, were most embraced in the writing, this linked the self with other people.

A broadening of the sphere of our self is an important way that positive emotions work for us – because it strengthens our connection with others. One participant, Jane, poignantly illuminated how writing can connect us to others.

A STORY OF WRITING LOVE

Jane was a mother of one who was home-schooling her teenage son. When she wrote with love, she described a conversation with her husband that was particularly poignant.

CASE STUDY

Jane

"I think when I wrote with love... my experience was that I didn't have any hard edges. So whereas I might have thought... my husband coming in and saying, "Oh, is there anything I can do to help with [dinner]?" when I've already done everything, if I wasn't writing about that with love, I could quite easily have gone into a judgemental place and thought... do you know, you always do that. You come in and you ask [laughs] if I want any help, when I've finished, or almost finished. And where I come from if I'm using a love filter is, nah, it's okay, I've done it – but you could make me a cup of tea." Jane also spoke about positive journalling in relation to the periods of depression she had been experiencing. "I think I was in a more positive frame of mind than when I started... There are always different ways to look at things... I get myself into a loop of negative thinking, and that 'poor me' place, and actually, if I catch myself early enough, I can get myself out of it... Having a positive focus and making that time to sit down and work with that, I think can only be helpful."

> *Writing might even have a profound impact on our relationships.*

In Jane's story, we can see that she did not simply react to a difficult situation with her husband by offloading it onto the page. Instead, she first reframed the situation and then changed her future actions to match this reframing. The positive emotion of love acted not only as a bridge connecting Jane and her partner, but as a bridge between her private writings and her real experiences. When she wrote with positive emotions, Jane described *acting* in line with what she had written. She became more "pro-social" in her behaviour, as well as increasing her sense of her own capability to handle a potentially aggravating incident with her husband. Through her writing, Jane both experienced self-expansion and strategized for the future. She built a bridge between her sphere of self on the page and the wider sphere of her world.

Combining positive emotions such as love with writing is a powerful synthesis. Writing might even have a profound impact on our relationships, including our romantic relationships. Researcher Richard Slatcher of the Close Relationships Laboratory at Wayne State University in Detroit, along with writing researcher James Pennebaker, found that writing expressively about our love lives might be of particular benefit to those in romantic relationships. In one study, they asked 86 dating couples to write their "deepest thoughts and feelings" about their relationships and found that the people who did so were much more likely still to be with their partners three months later, compared with those who did not write about their relationship.[35] When we write with love, our relationships with those we love can be made fundamentally stronger. This particular study suggested that writing increased emotional expressiveness between partners, and it was this that probably improved relationship stability. Another reason might be that writing with the emotion of love deepens our feeling of connection with others. Or perhaps a written focus on love simply prioritizes this emotion in our lives, making us more tolerant and making our relationship more stable.

This shows that when writing is used purposefully with a positive emotion such as love, as well as increasing emotional expressiveness, it might actually increase our feelings of connection with, and tolerance for, the other people in our lives.

Jane also stressed how writing with positive emotions such as love helped her to see things differently. Importantly, she said this was not like wearing "rose-tinted glasses, because that implies a lack of reality, but it is... a bit like taking a dirty pair of glasses off." Positive journalling is a reminder that, sometimes, an overtly negative or cynical response is inappropriate, even damaging – and may need to be "taken off" like a pair of smudged spectacles. When Jane wrote with love, this sense of reframing her more negative feelings supported her in what she described as "sitting down and working with" her emotions – in all their forms. Positive journalling is not about blindly revering positivity and happiness as the supreme human states. In fact, putting a high value on happiness, if we do not genuinely feel we have it, can sometimes be detrimental to our wellbeing.[36] We are not deficient if we are struggling to feel happy – to feel love, hope, serenity or any of the other emotions in this book. The truth is that most of us will struggle to access these emotions at times. Positive journalling is simply about making time to "sit down and work with" our emotions.

Jane's story shows that writing with love can be a way of noticing where this emotion might be hiding, underneath our habitual ways of looking at the world. Writing with love is taking the time to sit down and illuminate, compassionately and non-judgementally, our micro-experiences of positivity. In doing so, perhaps we can use our journals to put together, piece by piece, the beautiful puzzle of our happiness.

TAKEAWAY LESSONS

1 **WRITING WITH POSITIVE EMOTIONS CAN AFFECT OUR RELATIONSHIPS FOR THE BETTER.**

Stress, alarm clocks, coffee, commutes – all of these can leave us feeling pretty frazzled and not quite ourselves, and this can lead us to be not quite ourselves with other people. We can become grumpy and snappy. Positive emotions such as love redress the balance. They are excellent at linking us more strongly with others because, evolutionarily speaking, this is probably one of the most important functions positive emotions have had to fill.

2 **WRITING POSITIVELY IS NOT NECESSARILY ABOUT ADOPTING ROSE-TINTED GLASSES – IT CAN BE LIKE TAKING A PAIR OF DIRTY GLASSES OFF.**

Very often, we view positivity with cynicism, because we liken it to pushy "positive thinking" and shoehorning ourselves into a mood that is not coming easily. Yet positive journalling is not about applying a "happy" mood over our bad one, like layering dubious wallpaper over dubious wallpaper. Think of it rather as a stripping back of the viewpoints we are holding on to that might not be serving us. Anxiety, stress and other kinds of persistent negativity have a way of building up, like limescale in a kettle – or smudges on our glasses. Sometimes, micro-moments of positivity – in this case positive journal writing – can be one small way of clearing these away, to make space for an outlook that might just be far more useful to us.

3

POSITIVE JOURNALLING IS SIMPLY TIME TO SIT WITH ALL OF OUR EMOTIONS.

With sensitivity, self-compassion and the courage to ask others for help, writing this way can be a *supportive tool* in our low periods, as well as a constructive practice during happier times. If you have never attempted journal writing, think about it like talking to a counsellor or a close friend – someone reassuring who can be there to talk about whatever is going on for you, but who also helps you to spot unhelpful patterns, and opportunities to reframe outdated viewpoints.

TEN WAYS TO WRITE WITH **LOVE**

This is the final set of exercises that are yours to use in your own positive journalling practice. Think throughout these prompts about how you would like writing with love to extend beyond the page and into actions. You may want to keep in your mind's eye the image of love as a bridge between you and everything else.

As with the previous prompts, remember to be vivid in your detail and description, as well as sincere and authentic. If the writing ever feels false or forced, stop, take a pause and begin again, perhaps another day, once you can access some genuine feelings of love.

one

WRITE ABOUT A TIME IN THE PAST WHEN YOU FELT LOVE. This might be a big event like your wedding day, or something much smaller like a hug from a kind soul when you needed it most. Seek within your mental archives for times when love was extended to you, and you felt it reciprocally. Write in detail about why this was, how it felt and what it meant.

two

WRITE ABOUT A FUTURE TIME WHEN YOU ANTICIPATE YOU WILL FEEL LOVE. If you cannot think of a forthcoming occasion to write about, then you have the perfect excuse to get love in the diary! As the saying goes, love is a doing word and this mantra is by no means limited to romantic love. Although it might be a date night with your partner, it might also be coffee with a close friend where you commit to telling her how much she means to you; or ten minutes of loving-kindness meditation. Picture this scene and write about why prioritizing love in this way is important to you.

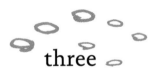

three

WRITE ABOUT YOUR LOVE IN THE PRESENT MOMENT. Rifle around in your heart as if it were a box of treasures in the attic and see what you find. Who do you feel the most love for in this instant? Why? How does it feel? If there is no particular person in your thoughts, you may want to write about love as a sense of benevolence toward all creatures, cultures and the planet. There is also nothing to stop you writing about the love you feel for yourself – we all need to hear this from ourselves sometimes. We are, after all, often our own harshest critics.

four

WRITE ABOUT A PERSON WHO MAKES YOU FEEL LOVE. This does not have to be a significant other. A loving parent, child, kind friend or anyone else who comes to mind is just as worthy of your affectionate reflections. Be sure not to leave it at "I care about them a lot" – instead, write about why the world is better with them in it, in tiny ways and larger ways. Love is the wellspring of most of the world's great art, literature, music and poetry, so you have no excuse not to get a little imaginative.

WRITE ABOUT WHAT LOVE FEELS LIKE, LOOKS LIKE, TASTES LIKE OR SMELLS LIKE. Building on the previous exercise, choose now to invite some metaphor into your writing, if you have not already done so. For singer Roberta Flack, the sun rose in the eyes of her lover. What a spectacularly precise metaphor for the tidal, all-encompassing feeling of falling in love. Is your love a clap of thunder or the soft touch of velvet? Does it taste of spicy chocolate-chilli or sustaining milk and honey? Get specific, have fun, be silly – words are instruments for exploring our emotions. Treat your writing as a jam session, not a test to compose a perfect concerto.

five

six

WRITE ABOUT HOW YOU COULD THINK OF LOVE DIFFERENTLY. Which experiences have you had that you could take a look at through the "lens" of love? Perhaps it is a scene of baking with an elderly family member, where no words were spoken but love filled the room like the scent of warm scones. Or maybe it was stopping to chat candidly with a homeless person and spare some change for them, where your love for humanity felt too great to just walk by. Love, like water, seeps into our lives through many cracks and crannies – sometimes so that it fills us to bursting point and we find ourselves deeply moved in an unexpected way. It is a dreadful cliché, but love is everywhere: in so many ways it is our drive and motivation, our reason for being and doing and seeking and settling down. Look for it and take note.

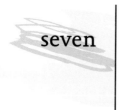

seven

WRITE ABOUT WHY OTHERS LOVE YOU. Tragically, many of us feel quite unlovable and are even surprised when someone expresses their love for us. Be reminded, however, that love does not have an entry exam. Love is not about being smart, or skinny, or successful, or sexy, or rich. Granted, these things might play a big part in attraction, novelty and passion – all the things that get love stirring – but they are not *it*. Love is about inner worlds and letting people catch a glimpse of ours. So, see if you can allow the internal Love Police to stand aside a second – to stop touting the "only skinny-me deserves love" or "only successful-me deserves love" missives – and focus on why others might love you, just as you are. This could be a life's work. It is worth it.

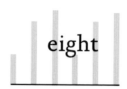

eight

WRITE ABOUT HOW YOU COULD BEGIN A DAILY PRACTICE OF LOVE. If we were all doing this, instead of practising the dog-eat-dog rules of modern life, what a profoundly different place this planet would be to live in. We may be going in the right direction, but there is still a long road to travel. Do your bit to take a few steps along that road. Start simply: write about how you might practise love with the people closest to you. Then extend this to a broader compassion for all things. This might come in the form of making a charitable donation or volunteering. It might be reading to a young or elderly relative and really being present with them – not rushing through or checking your phone every two seconds. Write about how you can love mindfully. Write about how you can love as if it matters (it is the only thing that really does for most of us, in the end). Write about how you could love a little bit more daily.

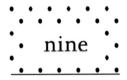

nine

WRITE ABOUT FEELING LOVE FOR YOUR SURROUNDINGS. There is that sensation when you see a little green shoot poke up through the soil and you want to do everything you can to help it grow (hopefully you have felt this – if not, then run-do-not-walk to your nearest vegetable garden). What is that feeling if not love? The desire to protect and preserve, even if it is ultimately futile – that is love. That is – at the risk of sounding grandiose – our humanity. Write about your love for the natural world and how you can help to care for it.

ten

WRITE ABOUT LOVE AS A BRIDGE. The theme of this chapter has been to think about how love and our other positive emotions help us in crossing boundaries – boundaries between page and world, and between self and other. How might this translate in your own life? Where has love served for you as a bridge? Maybe it has helped you to connect to another community or culture. Maybe it bonded you with others in an extremely testing time, like a death or crisis. Maybe it happens every day, in a million small ways, with your partner or a dear friend. Explore this in your writing.

CONCLUSION

Write on!

This book has highlighted some of the psychology behind positive journalling. This final chapter will tell a different story. Journal writing is also creative, an artful way of navigating our lives and a continual work in progress. These final pages extend the invitation for you to bring your own artistry and creativity to your journal writing.

A POSITIVE JOURNAL IS AN INVITATION TO BE CREATIVE

Whenever we are writing, we are creating. Even the most mundane piece of writing, such as an everyday email, can tend toward the creative. We think, "How should I say this?" or "Does this capture what I mean?" or even "Does this paint the right picture?"

Storytelling is one of the defining characteristics of being human. Journal writing is also a kind of storytelling: we are telling stories to ourselves! We are being creative – and this is one of the key ways we can look to journalling as an *art*.

Meaningfully wording our innermost thoughts and feelings as we do in journalling will usually involve some imagery or metaphor, because this is a natural characteristic of human language. We say things like "I feel down" as a metaphor for sadness or use the image of being "over the moon" with happiness. More than this, writing our experience in a seemingly factual way will usually include a kind of narrative or even plot – because we tend to order our experience like a story, in chronological order, listing key events not always as they happened, but by how important they were to the narrative we are trying to put together. These are features of creative writing. So we can begin to see how much creative artistry there already is in our journal writing. The trick is to acknowledge this and put it to good use.

The wonderful thing about acknowledging – and allowing for – artistry in our journal writing is that creativity allows us to be a bit messy. We can metaphorically get our paint-smudged aprons on and use the page as a proverbial canvas for sketching the person we might want to become (with many drafts!).

Journalling has long held this function – as a place to scribble our innermost thoughts without fear of judgement – but much modern-day journalling has become very rigid. Do a quick web search of "bullet journal" and you will find image after image of painstaking calligraphy and intricate watercolour illustrations. These impossibly high standards for our journals might prompt torn-out pages when we feel we do it wrong. But this idea – that we could possibly do a journal "wrong" – is a trap. It stops us gaining many of the feel-good benefits of journalling and might even make us feel like a failure if we do not live up to an ideal.

This showy approach to journalling is an understandable consequence of the incessant photo-snapping and sharing culture of the 21st century. Sharing our journals because they are beautiful is a great hobby, if we enjoy it, but we should also feel free to write without fearing the judgement of others. We should feel free to be messy – and to see the charm, beauty and plentiful potential in that mess.

A POSITIVE JOURNAL IS A WAY TO NAVIGATE OUR LIVES

The messier and more honest we are in our journalling, the better it serves us as a way of *navigating through life*. You might like to think of this by imagining each day of your life – perhaps each new encounter, each new idea or each new obligation – as a new tree that springs up along your path. Gradually, as you might expect, new trees obscure your view of the original trees. The new roots trip you up. The path is altered and you feel lost. Stopping to write is something akin to Hansel and Gretel's breadcrumb trail: it is keeping an eye on the path back home. It offers a broad perspective, so that one big, bushy new tree is not all that you see. You can also make out the breadcrumb path curling around its trunk and back off into the distant past. A journal helps you to recall all the other "trees" that felt impossibly dense and bushy, but that you passed on your route nonetheless.

What is important to note is that, when you write, you are remembering your past self, acknowledging your present self *and* sending a signal to your future self to say, "Hey, you! This is what that felt like." So writing in a journal is a way to keep a tab on any repetitive themes in your life. It is a way to give yourself advice, so that, when others give *their* advice, you can size it up against a more comprehensive picture of your life's mission, mistakes and marvels.

A POSITIVE JOURNAL
IS A WORK IN PROGRESS

We humans like to think of ourselves as *finished* works of art: neatly concluded portraits. We find an appealing world-view, set of circumstances or person; then we stamp it with our seal of approval, sit back and mistakenly think that things will stay the way they are. Often, life will have other plans for us. The reality is that, in much of our life experience, any such conclusions we arrive at about our lives are likely to be deceptive.

Any positive journal – just like any life – is a perpetual work in progress. But this is a good thing, because it offers us an invitation to what's possible. Far more important than any fixed conclusion (for example, to say boldly "I am happy" and put a full stop on the end) is the ability to be flexibly resilient and to marvel at possibility. Journalling is not necessarily a way to conclude or to *solve* anything, but only to buoy us up again and again on this wonderful, bumpy merry-go-round we call existence. Think about the contradictory title of this chapter: *Conclusion: Write On!* Put another way, the only conclusion you should take from this book is *not to seek conclusions* in your positive journalling, but just to keep on writing.

Conclusions may give us the sense that we have finally wrestled our lives into submission. Yet the reality is that we only ever exist in one tiny pixel of a much bigger picture. Life is fluid and evolving, and because of this nothing about it is ever truly conclusive. The philosopher Aristotle famously said that a happy life could only be judged in its entirety – in other words when it is literally over and we pass away. Therefore, Aristotle would say, it is a pretty pointless endeavour to grasp for happy conclusions until that point.

Instead of striving toward these happy conclusions, then, what if we actively made a happy life, daily? This idea is at the heart of positive journalling. Our micro-moments of positive emotion are fleeting. For this reason, we should never give up the reins of our happiness to a comfortable conclusion – rather, we should treat happiness like a verb: a doing word.

We should aim not to arrive at happiness or even to *be* happy, but to *do* happy. Positive psychology shows that intentional activity is one of the biggest impacts we can have on our wellbeing. The trick, both with journalling and with living the story of our lives, is to engage – actively and dynamically. We must stay at the artist's easel, not drop our paintbrush for the sake of a neat conclusion. This is the only real way to write ourselves happy: to use journal writing as a process of staying continually engaged with our wellbeing, and the wellbeing of those around us.

WHERE NEXT FOR YOUR POSITIVE JOURNAL PRACTICE?

This final chapter has offered a manifesto to help you treat your journal writing like an art form: a messy yet beautiful work in progress. Whereas the previous chapters offered guided routes into positive journalling, this chapter has been a gentle nudge off piste, toward your own creative freestyle. Not quite there yet? No matter. Revisit this book. Scribble in its margins. Rip out whole pages and ceremoniously burn them if need be. Just be sure to do one thing: keep on writing. Whether you call it positive journalling or something else. Keep writing. Whether you do it Diary-capital-D style in a clothbound tome or with a felt-tip on a bit of ripped-off cereal box. Keep writing. Whether you schedule it to the minute like a German rail network or write with erratic, wanton spontaneity. Just. Keep. Writing.

Yet – whenever and however you choose to write – commit to making your journal a positive force in your life (whatever this *truly* means to you). In this book I have suggested that a good way to begin is to be anchored by your innate, authentic, positive emotions. This is because when we write with positive emotions, a whole world of alternative perspectives opens up – perspectives that might be far more helpful and comforting than even the most time-honoured outlook we have held on life. When we write in this way, we do not just feel relieved – we feel a sense of progress in our writing. The page becomes a bridge to real change. When we write in this way, writing can make us happier.

ENDNOTES

1 Megan C. Hayes and Kate Hefferon, "Not like rose-tinted glasses... like taking a pair of dirty glasses off": A pilot intervention using positive emotions in expressive writing". *International Journal of Wellbeing* 5, no. 4, (December 2015): 78–95.

2 Martin E. P. Seligman, Tayyab Rashid and Acacia C. Parks, "Positive Psychotherapy", *American Psychologist* 61, no. 8 (2006): 774–88.

3 Barbara L. Fredrickson, "Learning to Self-Generate Positive Emotions", in *Changing Emotions*, ed. Dirk Hermans, Bernard Rimé and Batja Mesquita (Psychology Press, 2013), 151–156.

4 James W. Pennebaker and Joshua M. Smyth, *Opening Up by Writing It Down: How Expressive Writing Improves Health and Eases Emotional Pain* (Guilford Press, 2016).

5 Within the broadly defined field of writing and wellbeing, there are some notable "contraindications" (contradictory findings) against the suggestion that writing always supports mental health, which we would be remiss to ignore. For a discussion of these, see: Jeannie Wright and Man Cheung Chung, "Mastery or Mystery? Therapeutic Writing: A Review of the Literature". *British Journal of Guidance and Counselling* 29, no. 3 (2001): 277–291.

6 Alvin Poon and Sharon Danoff-Burg, "Mindfulness as a Moderator in Expressive Writing", *Journal of Clinical Psychology* 67, no. 9 (2011): 881–895.

7 Chad M. Burton and Laura A. King, "The Health Benefits of Writing about Intensely Positive Experiences", *Journal of Research in Personality* 38, no. 2 (2004): 150–163.

8 Laura A. King and Kathi N. Miner, "Writing about the Perceived Benefits of Traumatic Events: Implications for Physical Health", *Personality and Social Psychology Bulletin* 26, no. 2 (2000): 220–230.

9 James W. Pennebaker and Sandra K. Beall, "Confronting a Traumatic Event: Toward an Understanding of Inhibition and Disease", *Journal of Abnormal Psychology* 95, no. 3 (1986): 274–281.

10 Alice M. Isen and Paula F. Levin, "Effect of Feeling Good on Helping: Cookies and Kindness", *Journal of Personality and Social Psychology* 21, no. 3 (1972): 384–88.

11 Kareem J. Johnson and Barbara L. Fredrickson, "'We All Look the Same to Me': Positive Emotions Eliminate the Own-Race Bias in Face Recognition", *Psychological Science* 16, no. 11 (2005): 875–881.

12 Michael A. Cohn et al., "Happiness Unpacked: Positive Emotions Increase Life Satisfaction by Building Resilience", *Emotion* 9, no. 3 (2009): 361–68.

13 Barbara L. Fredrickson, "Positive Emotions Broaden and Build", in *Advances in Experimental Social Psychology*, vol. 47 (Academic Press, 2013), 2.

14 James W. Pennebaker and Cindy K. Chung, "Expressive Writing, Emotional Upheavals, and Health", in *Handbook of Health Psychology*, 2007, 263–284.

15 James W. Pennebaker quoted in Anna North, "How Keeping a Diary Can Surprise You", *The New York Times: The Opinion Pages* (September 2014).

16 Ting Zhang et al., "A 'Present' for the Future: The Unexpected Value of Rediscovery", *Psychological Science* 25, no. 10 (2014): 1851–1860.

17 Fredrickson, "Positive Emotions Broaden and Build", 4.

18 Robert A. Emmons and Michael E. McCullough, "Counting Blessings versus Burdens: An Experimental Investigation of Gratitude and Subjective Well-Being in Daily Life", *Journal of Personality and Social Psychology* 84, no. 2 (2003): 377–89.

19 Fredrickson, "Positive Emotions Broaden and Build", 4.

20 Marvin Levine, *The Positive Psychology of Buddhism and Yoga: Paths to a Mature Happiness*, second edition (Routledge, 2009), 5.

21 Ambra Burls, "People and Green Spaces: Promoting Public Health and Mental Well-Being through Ecotherapy", *Journal of Public Mental Health* 6, no. 3 (2007): 24–39.

22 Fredrickson, "Positive Emotions Broaden and Build," 4.

23 Paul J. Silvia, "Interest – The Curious Emotion", *Current Directions in Psychological Science* 17, no. 1 (2008): 57–60.

24 Fredrickson, "Positive Emotions Broaden and Build," 4.

25 Hubert J. M. Hermans, "The Construction and Reconstruction of a Dialogical Self", *Journal of Constructivist Psychology* 16, no. 2 (2003): 91.

26 Fredrickson, "Positive Emotions Broaden and Build", 4.

27 Charles R. Snyder, Kevin L. Rand and David R. Sigmon, "Hope Theory", in *Handbook of Positive Psychology*, ed. Charles R. Snyder and Shane J. Lopez, first edition (Oxford University Press, 2002), 258.

28 June Price Tangney and Kurt W. Fischer, eds., *Self-Conscious Emotions: The Psychology of Shame, Guilt, Embarrassment, and Pride* (Guilford Press, 1995).

29 Jessica L. Tracy and Richard W. Robins, "The Psychological Structure of Pride: A Tale of Two Facets", *Journal of Personality and Social Psychology* 92, no. 3 (2007): 506–525.

30 Fredrickson, "Positive Emotions Broaden and Build", 6.

31 Fredrickson, "Positive Emotions Broaden and Build", 6.

32 Dacher Keltner and Jonathan Haidt, "Approaching Awe, a Moral, Spiritual, and Aesthetic Emotion", *Cognition and Emotion* 17, no. 2 (2003): 297–314.

33 Fredrickson, *Love 2.0: Finding Happiness and Health in Moments of Connection* (Plume, 2014).

34 Fredrickson, "Positive Emotions Broaden and Build", 6.

35 Richard B. Slatcher and James W. Pennebaker, "How Do I Love Thee? Let Me Count the Words: The Social Effects of Expressive Writing", *Psychological Science* 17, no. 8 (2006): 660–664.

36 Iris B. Mauss et al., "Can Seeking Happiness Make People Unhappy? Paradoxical Effects of Valuing Happiness", *Emotion* 11, no. 4 (2011): 807–815.

FURTHER READING

Cameron, Julia, *The Artist's Way: A Course in Discovering and Recovering Your Creative Self* (Macmillan, 2016)

Fredrickson, Barbara, *Love 2.0: Finding Happiness and Health in Moments of Connection* (Plume, 2014)

Fredrickson, Barbara, *Positivity: Groundbreaking Research to Release Your Inner Optimist and Thrive* (Oneworld Publications, 2011)

Haidt, Jonathan, *The Happiness Hypothesis: Putting Ancient Wisdom to the Test of Modern Science* (Arrow, 2007)

Levine, Marvin, *The Positive Psychology of Buddhism and Yoga: Paths to a Mature Happiness* (Routledge, 2009)

Pennebaker, James, and Smyth, Joshua, *Opening Up by Writing It Down: How Expressive Writing Improves Health and Eases Emotional Pain* (Guilford Press, 2016)

Rainer, Tristine, *The New Diary: How to Use a Journal for Self-Guidance and Expanded Creativity (Jeremy P. Tarcher/ Penguin, 2004)*

Ricard, Matthieu, *Happiness: A Guide to Developing Life's Most Important Skill* (Atlantic Books, 2015)

Seligman, Martin, *Flourish: A New Understanding of Happiness and Well- Being – and How To Achieve Them* (Nicholas Brealey Publishing, 2011)

THE POSITIVE JOURNALLING STUDY

Hayes, M. C. and Hefferon, K. (2015) "Not like rose-tinted glasses... like taking a pair of dirty glasses off": A pilot intervention using positive emotions in expressive writing. *International Journal of Wellbeing.* 5(4), 78–95

RESOURCES

Enjoyed reading this book?

Want to learn more about writing for happiness?

Using positive emotions is just the start when it comes to a Positive Journal® practice. If you would like to learn more about developing your journal writing with the science of positive psychology, you will find further hints, practical tips and printable worksheets at:

www.positivejournal.org

If you would like to get in touch with Megan or follow her latest research and work, you can also visit her main website and say hello (she would love to hear from you!)

www.meganchayes.com

INDEX

ACKNOWLEDGEMENTS

There are so very many people involved in bringing any book into the world, and this one certainly took a village. The study at the heart of the book was made possible by the generous souls who took part, known by the pseudonyms of Valerie, Amanda, Louise, Laura, John, Rita, Mark, Jane, Rose, and Becky. I feel so privileged to have been gifted your time and candour through our conversations – your involvement made this study (and this book) a possibility, and a joy. My deep thanks also for the direction, expertise, and cheerleading of Kate Hefferon. I am honoured to have worked so closely with such an excellent researcher; your passion and reassurance throughout my MSc studies helped to transform me from student to bona fide researcher. A hearty thank you is of course due to my agent, Jane Graham-Maw, for your shrewd advice, dedication, and belief in my ideas. I am grateful to the team at Octopus, in particular to Leanne Bryan for your warm encouragement and enthusiastic commitment to this project. Thank you to Alex Stetter for your tireless effort in bringing the many elements of the book together, and for involving me so closely at every stage. My deep thanks will always be due to Sophie Nicholls for your warm mentorship and for helping to initiate me into the working worlds of academia and publishing alike – you are an inspiration. Thank you, also, to my many other dear colleagues and friends – your presence in my life has helped me to develop as a person and a writer: Kristen Truempy, Susanna Halonen, Carles Torra, Ellen Grant, Hannah Milton, Jenny Lovino, Lauren Gurteen, Kathleen Tompsett, Grace Parker, Saleem Ansari, Catherine Gilbert, and Eleanor Marsea. Thank you to my maternal grandmother, Theolyn Cortens, for always offering a model of brave creativity, and also to my inspiring grandfather, Will Shaman. My formative conversations with each of you throughout my life have helped me believe in my own creations. Thanks, of course, to dear Grandma Eileen – you have always radiated happiness and are a true inspiration to me. Thank you to my brother-in-law, John Pingstone, for reading early drafts of this book and for never being afraid to provide honest criticism. Finally, my eternal gratitude goes to my immediate family, who are the wind in the sails of everything I do. My mum and dad, Tamsin and Sean Hayes, my sister, Alice Pingstone, and my remarkable little niece Xanthe Pingstone – thank you all, always, for everything.